You and Your Hearing-Impaired Child

A Self-Instructional Guide for Parents

John W. Adams

Illustrations by Susie Duckworth

Clerc Books
Gallaudet University Press
Washington, D. C.

Clerc Books
An imprint of Gallaudet University Press
Washington, DC 20002

Published 1988; Second printing 1991
Printed in the United States of America

Library of Congress Cataloging-in-Publication Data

Adams, John W., 1956-
    You and your hearing-impaired child

    Bibliography: p.
    1. Parents of handicapped children—United States.
2. Parenting—United States.   3. Children, Deaf—
United States—Family relationships.   4. Hearing
impaired children—United States—Family Relationships.
I. Title
HQ759.913.A33 1988 649'.1512 88-29948
ISBN 0-930323-40-8

Cover illustration and design by Susie Duckworth.

To my parents, who have a special way of
making others feel happy.

Table of Contents

Acknowledgments

You and Your Hearing-Impaired Child was originally conceived as a parent education manual to provide parents with a practical guide they could use with their hearing-impaired children. Through the contributions of many special people, this initial effort has now grown into a book.

I am deeply grateful to all of the parents who gave their time, efforts, and input during the initial stages of the book's development. They have enriched my life.

I owe much to my mentor and colleague, Dr. Romeria Tidwell, who has touched my life with her encouragement, support, and professional expertise. I will always be grateful that our paths crossed.

My appreciation goes out to my friends and colleagues who offered me patience and understanding. Their love and support helped me endure.

I owe a special debt of gratitude to Starr Richardson, who contributed hours of commitment and enthusiasm while typing and preparing several drafts of this book.

I also wish to thank the staff of Gallaudet University Press, who used great care in preparing my book for publication. Special thanks to Ivey Pittle, the managing editor, whose thoughtful input was indeed effective in improving the contents of this book.

And lastly, I extend my deepest appreciation to my family: Mary Ann, Bill, Mark, Tom, Nancy, and Tina. Their support provided me with laughter and strength. And to my mother and father, Mary and Bill Adams—I am truly blessed by their infinite love, faith, and encouragement.

CHAPTER ONE

An Introduction

This book is intended for parents of hearing-impaired children. Some of you will be reading this book after you first discover that your child is hearing-impaired, others will have had experienced the impact of hearing impairment on your child and family for years. In any case, this book is about you, your child, and how you interact together. By using this book, you will learn more about yourself and about your hearing-impaired child. In reading this book, you have made a commitment to understand more about your child, yourself, and your family. You have made a commitment of caring and of love.

While the following pages can be useful to all parents of hearing-impaired youngsters, those having children newly diagnosed with a hearing disability may find the contents particularly helpful.

You and Your Hearing-Impaired Child consists of eleven chapters. Each chapter is designed to provide information of importance to parents of hearing-impaired children. Chapters two and three include material on feelings about hearing impairment and a discussion of how to cope with these feelings. Chapter four introduces the topic of "normal" child development and how hearing impairment can affect behavior. Chapters five, six, and seven involve managing your hearing-impaired child's behavior through general limit setting or programs specifically designed to stop unwanted behaviors. Chapter eight contains vital information on nonverbal communication and the role it plays in the lives of hearing-impaired children. Developing plans for solving future problems is discussed in chapter nine. Presented in chapter ten are general topics of concern regarding hearing impairment such as language development, choice of communication method, and appropriate education placement. The book concludes with a final chapter listing references and general resources for parents. You can use these sources to learn more about hearing impairment or to obtain help in specific areas of concern.

Chapters two through eight follow a seven-section format:

Introduction includes a description of the concepts and skills to be introduced.

Skill Development includes a review of the information in the previous chapter and the skills and concepts to be learned in the present chapter.

Applications includes a description of the impact of hearing impairment on the material covered. It also includes a discussion of how the information presented can be used with a hearing-impaired child.

Parent and Child includes interactions and statements showing the appropriate use of skills, principles, and concepts presented.

Points to Remember includes a summary of all important points made throughout the chapter.

Activities for Practice includes activities and exercises so that you can practice the skills you have learned.

Checking Your Progress includes an evaluation of your progress and a check on your understanding of the information presented. Problem situations and questions requiring your response are provided.

You are encouraged to read each chapter carefully, do the activities, and finally complete the "Checking Your Progress" section. Chapters two through eight provide feedback for your work. Typical responses to the "Activities for Practice" and answers to the "Checking Your Progress" are provided at the end of this book.

The length of time it will take you to complete the book depends on many factors—your time, energy, effort, and most important, your understanding about hearing impairment and how it affects you and your child. It is important to know that wherever you are at this moment—you are. Take the time necessary to truly grasp and work through the material in each chapter.

Many books are read, put away, and forgotten. *You and Your Hearing-Impaired Child* is not like other books. You can keep it near, review it, and use it again and again, depending on your needs. In time your thoughts, ideas, and opinions may change. My intent is that parents of hearing-impaired children use the material in this book continuously.

Finally, as you read the following pages, you may need to discuss your reactions and responses to the content with someone else. Parents have used many sources when discussing the material, including friends, family members, other parents of hearing-impaired children, and professionals such as clergy, counselors, audiologists, and doctors.

It is my hope that you will find *You and Your Hearing-Impaired Child* helpful, informative, and important in your daily interactions with your child and family.

CHAPTER TWO

Hearing Impairment— Becoming Aware of Your Feelings

INTRODUCTION

Learning that your child is hearing-impaired can be frightening. It is common for parents to experience some difficulty in learning to accept their child's hearing loss. You may be prepared for the diagnosis after making many visits to doctors and from tests you perform at home. But, the awful moment when it is confirmed that *your* child is hearing-impaired triggers feelings and thoughts that are equal to no other.

Following the diagnosis of hearing impairment, parents generally experience a range of feelings. Many parents find themselves going through stages of emotions which may include sadness, anxiety, confusion, and depression. These feelings are normal, and they are temporary. But although these feelings are natural, they can interfere with the way you interact with your child. This chapter, "Hearing Impairment—Becoming Aware of Your Feelings," is designed to point out the stages parents generally move through, focusing on the reactions of parents of hearing-impaired children.

As you read this chapter and practice the exercises presented at the end, please make an effort to remember the feelings you had when you first learned of your child's hearing loss. Also make an effort to remember how your feelings influenced your actions with your child. Some of you are still in the process of accepting your child's hearing impairment. For others, the information provided in this chapter will be a reminder of the past. In either case, what is important is that *you* are aware of when you are experiencing certain feelings and of how these may influence the interaction between you and your child.

Skill Development

Many parents say that they experienced very powerful emotions during the period of time surrounding the diagnosis of their child's handicap. Unfortunately, there is no set formula for dealing with such strong emotions. Individuals handle situations differently. The diagnosis of a handicapping condition in a child generally brings forth from parents reactions that are similar to those experienced by persons who have lost something of extreme value. When you lose something that is important to you—such as a loved one, your health, your job, or your dreams of the future—you will naturally experience a period of *mourning*. Mourning is the behavior we use to express sorrow or grief (Hubler, 1983). The way you mourn usually depends on the way your parents have mourned and on your culture. But people do go through several stages as they grieve a loss. Becoming aware of the stages of grief and learning to recognize what stage you are in may make it easier for you to cope with mourning.

The Three Stages of Grief

The first reaction to the discovery of your loss is shock. Why? Because you now know you have a child who does not fit your expectations. There is a loss. As the initial shock lessens, you begin to experience strong emotions such as anger, sadness, and finally, denial. It is common not to want to believe this has happened to you, to your child, or to your family.

During this stage you recognize that your child has a disability. Not everyone experiences all of the emotions that characterize this stage. You may have personally experienced only a few of them. They include sadness, anxiety, anger, guilt, shame, blame, disappointment, hurt, bewilderment, confusion, helplessness, loneliness, hope, and relief. Eventually these feelings decrease in frequency, strength, and the amount of disruption they cause in your life (Hubler, 1983).

During the recovery stage, you accept your child's condition. Acceptance does not mean being content with your situation, but it means you are better able to cope with the handicapping condition. What you learned during the two earlier stages helps you to deal with your feelings and to adapt to your situation. You are now better able to accept your new role as a parent of a disabled youngster.

Feelings are neither good nor bad. They are simply feelings. It may be harmful to pretend that they do not exist. When we ignore feelings such as disappointment, anxiety, rejection, and guilt, troublesome feelings and attitudes can develop (Green, 1971). Knowing and accepting that feelings exist is a step that can enable you to move forward. Being aware of your feelings can help you gain more control over them. Gaining control of your feelings will help give you more energy to act and do something about your situation.

It is important to know that the stages of the mourning process are not perfectly separated. Each stage cannot be clearly defined as having specific behaviors associated only with it. For example, sometimes you may believe you are experiencing feelings and behaving like you are in the recovery stage, but from time to time you may experience strong emotions usually seen at the recognition stage. It is quite normal, at times, to go back through phases of the mourning process.

Also, you may not experience feelings or behaviors common to a particular stage. For instance, you may accept the diagnosis or the implications of the handicapping condition in the early phases. On the other hand, you may have feelings about your child's handicapping condition, but not experience strong emotions. Again, parents' reactions to the diagnosis of a handicap in their children differ.

Finally, the period of time spent in one stage or another varies from individual to individual. The length of time will depend on many factors. Ways of coping used, past experiences, and attitudes can all dictate the amount of time spent at a certain stage. What is important to understand is that the rate you go through this process can differ from others around you. At one extreme, you may adapt to your new situation quickly, say in a few months. At the other extreme, you may move very slowly, feeling stuck with a feeling of little hope. Most parents move slowly forward, experiencing and re-experiencing strong feelings and learning new ways of coping (Boothroyd, 1982).

> **Third Stage: Recovery**

> *Most parents move slowly forward, experiencing and re-experiencing strong feelings and learning new ways of coping .*

Applications

Accepting your feelings about hearing impairment is a movement toward understanding what is presently occurring with your family and what might occur in the future. Feelings are very real when they happen, but they are also temporary. Feelings of pride and accomplishment often replace those of worry and fear (*Correspondence Course*, 1983). For example, as time goes on you may still experience disappointment or fear when your child is attempting something new. However, happy experiences you have had with your hearing-impaired child can lessen the impact of problematic feelings. Let us now examine the stages of grief as they relate to parents of hearing-impaired children.

Prediagnosis Phase

In the prediagnosis phase, the family has a suspicion that something is wrong. The full impact is yet to be felt because the diagnosis is yet to be confirmed (Goldberg, 1979). Many times you feel alone during this phase as you try to convince others that something is wrong. When your anxiety can no longer be avoided or denied, you begin the difficult task of confirming your suspicions about your child.

Doctors and professionals often remain distant and express views that you are an over-anxious parent. They may even say, "Nothing is wrong!" Finally, sometimes after days, weeks, or months of anxiety-provoking visits to doctors or professionals, the words "Your child has a hearing loss" are spoken. Now the painful reality hits. Shock sets in.

Diagnosis Phase

The diagnosis phase is characterized by a feeling of shock. Shock is a temporary state that passes into anxiety, fear, and often panic. During the diagnosis phase, it is difficult to make specific plans. Both parents may be faced with feelings ranging from guilt about being responsible for their child's handicap to temporary happiness due to fantasizing about having a normal hearing child. But the reality of the child's handicap does not disappear and it must be handled. You may decide that denial is the best way to cope with this situation. Coping through denial may help for a short while. Denial serves a distinct and important purpose (Moses, 1985). It helps you cope with danger or difficult times by offering temporary protection against harm. Denying the handicap is a way to avoid the painful feelings and the reality of the diagnosis. You may need time to understand and adapt to what just occurred—the diagnosis of hearing impairment. You may use denial to buy the time needed to find strength and determine other ways of coping (e.g., gathering information, gaining support from friends, developing a sense of belongingness through membership in organizations, etc.). But denial is neither constructive nor helpful when you use it continuously to avoid or ignore doing something about the situation.

An important factor in coping within the diagnosis phase is the knowledge of the etiology of hearing impairment—the cause of the hearing impairment. Not knowing the cause of hearing loss can be a source of anxiety for parents. This anxiety may affect your attitudes and treatment toward your hearing-impaired child (Meadow, 1980). It is helpful for you to understand the cause of your child's hearing loss. This knowledge reduces the tendency for you to blame yourself (Mindel & Vernon, 1987).

The diagnosis phase is characterized by a feeling of shock.

People have several misconceptions about the reasons for a hearing loss, ranging from a blow to the head to "brain fever." These typical ideas about the origins of hearing impairment do not offer a true explanation for a loss of hearing. In reality, there are several different possible causes, any of which could be the very reason for your child's hearing loss. Causes of hearing loss include heredity, blood incompatibility, accidents, drugs, poisons, allergies, bacterial infections (e.g., meningitis), viral infections (e.g., mumps, rubella, measles), and birth accidents (e.g., prematurity, birth injury) (Quigley & Kretschmer, 1982).

Knowing the reason for the hearing loss can help you to cope with the situation (Meadow, 1968). It can relieve the tension of not knowing what caused your child's disability. It is important to know, however, that for a large number of hearing-impaired children (one-third), the cause is unknown (Meadow, 1980). The unknown category is currently larger than any single known cause of hearing impairment.

Hearing impairments arise from many causes, some of which are known and others not known (Brown, 1986). In any case, learning the facts about your child's hearing loss is important. You can shorten the period of your recovery from the diagnosis of hearing loss in your child with accurate knowledge and information (McArthur, 1982).

Postdiagnosis Phase

Once you acknowledge the hearing loss, denial and pain will decrease and acceptance will begin. The road to acceptance is not easy. Initially, you may be forced into accepting your child's hearing disability. When the reality of hearing loss is present, true mourning begins and the greatest loss is felt (Goldberg, 1979). As previously noted, it is very important to remember that you may go through different stages of the mourning process, and you may use different ways of coping with your feelings than other parents. You may want to discuss and talk through feelings, while another parent may keep feelings inside and find them difficult to discuss. After time, the feeling of crisis fades and healing starts. This period is the beginning of constructive acceptance. Healing can start by your coming to know your child as he or she is. At this time, you learn and practice coping behaviors so you can meet the needs of your child (Boothroyd, 1982).

Denial and learning the causes of hearing loss were mentioned as ways of coping in the diagnosis phase. You can develop a variety of ways to cope when dealing with the impact of hearing loss on your life and the life of your child following the diagnosis of hearing impairment. Understanding hearing loss and how it influences the behavior and the life of your child helps you to have hope in the future. The following chapters provide information to aid in your understanding about hearing loss and your child and can be used to help you cope. For now, let us discuss further helpful ways of coping.

As a human being and a parent, your development is a continuous process. To develop means to change and grow. From time to time, these changes are too sudden, too great, or too unwanted, and you cannot adapt quickly enough (Boothroyd, 1982). Having a hearing-impaired child presents a time of great change for parents. People use various ways of coping in order to deal with the abrupt changes in their lives. Gathering information and talking to family or friends about the situation are ways of coping in a healthy way. It may be necessary to include outside support to help in the coping process. Participating in individual counseling, support groups, or visits to clergy available in the community are effective ways to deal with this new situation.

It is important to keep in mind that as you develop, you continue to discover new ways of coping. Being aware of your feelings is one way to begin to deal with the changes in your life and the life of your child. In time you can use these newfound coping strategies to move ahead, survive, and grow. Developing specific coping strategies will be discussed in chapter three.

The Future

You may experience frustration from time to time. Being aware of this feeling will help guide you so you will not act for the wrong reasons. Frustration and grieving may recur in the future. As you grow, in time, you may experience loss. The grieving process is far from being a one-time occurrence. Each time your child comes to a major life milestone, it may impact you in a new way—and you may mourn again. For example, you may experience intense emotions when your hearing-impaired child begins school for the first time. You may compare your child with hearing children and the differences you discover may bring about sadness. Experiencing feelings and being aware of them is experiencing growth.

Every major change in the development of your child will demand adjustment. For example, puberty brings about dramatic changes in your child's physical, emotional, and social development. These changes present parents of all children—hearing or nonhearing—with dilemmas. But these dilemmas are more complex when a handicap involving communication is present. Explaining the changes in growth to your child will be more difficult.

Even the most subtle challenges may demand adjustment. For instance, listening to other parents discuss their children's accomplishments and growth may be a reminder of the differences between your child and others. Or needing to explain why a particular boy or girl who may not understand hearing loss did not choose your child as a close companion can bring about sadness or even anger.

The feeling that we are different from our children and that they are different from us is sometimes painful. Every parent experiences this feeling. Parents of hearing children experience this realization slowly as time proves this truth. Parents of hearing-impaired children, however, are shown this difference more harshly and abruptly (Kretschmer & Kretschmer, 1979). The difference need only be that this child is unique. Your child maintains the uniqueness of his or her own personality and the ability to give and receive love. The main difference between your child and any other is that your child is unable to hear.

Acceptance of your child's hearing-impaired condition does not mean you like it, welcome it, or prefer it. Acceptance means you understand and accept the reality that your child is and always will

Gathering information and talking to family or friends about the situation are ways of coping in a healthy way.

The main difference between your child and any other is that your child is unable to hear.

be hearing-impaired (Hubler, 1983). Acceptance means that you recognize that hearing impairment does make your child different, but your life need not center on this aspect. Being hearing-impaired, a child will have to work harder in the area of language. This can be an accepted part of the child's life; however, this fact should not prevent parents and others from communicating with the child. A form of communication best suited to the needs of the child and family can be developed. Hearing impairment does put realistic obstacles in the path of your child's development, but it should not be the focus in preventing your child and family from growing, developing, and sharing happiness.

Parent and Child

Listed below are examples of remarks parents have shared regarding the feelings experienced while moving through the stages of grief (partially adapted from Hubler, 1983, pp. 5–6):

Shock: "It was a shock to hear about John's deafness—I was stunned."

Denial: "A miracle will happen." "There must be a mistake about the diagnosis."

Sadness: "When I hear the birds chirping or a pretty song, I want Suzie to hear it too." "We will never be a normal family again!"

Anxiety: "Why did this happen to me?" "This child will always be a burden."

Guilt: "Did I do something wrong while I was pregnant?" "How can I make this up to my child?"

Shame: "His father pushes him aside and never wants to do anything for this child."

Blame: "We never expected deafness—I wonder whose fault it is?"

Disappointment: "He will never be the son that I wanted him to be."

Hurt: "It hurts; Selma said that her daughter is reading above grade level now."

Bewilderment: "I don't understand what deafness is all about, I don't even know any deaf people!"

Helplessness: "Nothing I can do will make a difference, I feel like giving up."

Loneliness: "Nobody knows what this is like. No one can help."

Acceptance: "Now that I know Tim is hearing-impaired, the next step is to find out what it really means." "Ken is deaf but he is normal in every way—he plays with the dog, is happy to see me and Dad, and is a crazy kind of kid."

Points to Remember

1. The diagnosis of a handicapping condition in a child generally brings forth from parents reactions that are similar to those experienced by persons who have lost something of extreme value. When you lose something that is important to you—such as a loved one, your health, your job, or your dreams of the future—you naturally experience a period of mourning.

2. Following the diagnosis of hearing impairment, parents go through stages in which many feelings are experienced, including sadness, anxiety, confusion, and depression. Such feelings are normal, and they are temporary.

3. What is important is that you are aware of when you are experiencing certain feelings and of how these feelings may influence the interactions between you and your child.

4. There are three stages of grief.

   First stage: Shock. Initial reaction of disbelief.

   Second stage: Recognition. Recognition of the condition. Painful feelings such as anger, sadness, guilt, fear, confusion, and helplessness may surface.

   Third stage: Recovery. Acceptance of the handicapping condition. Acceptance of the new role as a parent of a disabled youngster occurs.

5. Feelings are aroused throughout the prediagnosis (isolation and anxiety), diagnosis (shock, sadness, anger), and postdiagnosis (anger, sadness, despair lessens—acceptance begins) phases for the parents of hearing-impaired children.

6. Acceptance of your child's hearing-impaired condition does not mean you like it, welcome it, or prefer it. Acceptance means you understand and accept the reality that your child is and always will be hearing-impaired.

7. The hearing-impaired child maintains the uniqueness of his or her own personality and the ability to give and receive love. The main difference between your child and any other is that your child is unable to hear.

> *Acceptance means you understand and accept the reality that your child is and always will be hearing-impaired.*

Activities for Practice

Be sure to include the feelings you experience as you watch your child.

1. Take two ten-minute periods during the day to observe your child.
   a. Watch your child playing alone. The best time may be during playtime, resttime, or when your child is working. Write down your reactions about what you observe.

   _____

   _____

   _____

   _____

   _____

   _____

   _____

   _____

   _____

   b. Watch your child interacting with someone else. This may be done when your child is at the dinner table, is playing, etc. The interaction may involve siblings, friends, a parent, etc. Write down your reactions about what you observe.

Be sure to include the feelings that you experience as you watch the interaction.

   _____

   _____

   _____

   _____

   _____

   _____

   _____

   _____

   _____

2. Take about ten to fifteen minutes in a quiet place to reflect on your reaction when you found out that your child was hearing-impaired. Write down the feelings that you experienced. Also write down advice to parents who are in a similar situation.

Dear _____,

Write this in the form of a letter to yourself to remind yourself of what you learned from that experience.

_____

_____

_____

_____

_____

_____

_____

_____

_____

_____

_____

_____

_____

_____

_____

_____

_____

_____

Sincerely,

_____

3. It is important to understand how you handle grief and mourning or other events involving strong feelings. Several different types of feelings are listed below. When these feelings are very strong, how do you handle them?

Feeling	How I Handle This Feeling
depression	_____
	_____
	_____
anger	_____
	_____
	_____
loneliness	_____
	_____
	_____
helplessness	_____
	_____
	_____

4. Now that you have written down how you usually handle strong emotions, ask yourself this: Did any of your responses mention expressing these feelings to another person? If not, is there a person with whom you could share your feelings or experiences that cause such feelings? In the space below, list people you can turn to during particular times of need and how they may be reached. Sharing your feelings with another, be it a spouse, friend, clergy, or another parent of a hearing-impaired child, is an important practice for coping with experiences and the feelings these experiences bring about.

_____

_____

_____

_____

_____

_____

1. Read the sample problem below. Write down how you would handle this situation. What would you tell your child?

   Your child, who is about seven years old, comes home and asks, "Why am I different from other kids? Why am I hearing-impaired?"

   _____

   _____

   _____

   _____

   _____

   _____

   _____

   _____

   _____

   _____

2. True or False

   _____ a. Following the diagnosis of hearing impairment, parents generally experience reactions similar to those experienced from a loss of something important.

   _____ b. Experiencing intense emotions is common when parents are in the first stage of the grieving process— the initial stage of shock.

   _____ c. The feelings experienced by parents as they progress through stages to acceptance are negative feelings and must be worked through quickly in order to get on with life.

   _____ d. The feelings during stages of grieving that you experience in reaction to deafness can recur as your child and your family face new challenges and new experiences.

   _____ e. Acceptance of the hearing-impaired condition means that eventually you will be happy and content about this condition in your child.

   _____ f. You can rest assured that most parents of hearing-impaired children experience feelings and emotions similar to those you experience and that these feelings are natural and temporary.

CHAPTER THREE

Reactions to Hearing Impairment

We eventually learn that when our world suddenly changes it is possible to rebuild a new one.

INTRODUCTION

Chapter two presented information about feelings that you may experience during and surrounding the period of the diagnosis of hearing impairment in your child. These feelings are normal and temporary. As time goes on, however, your hearing-impaired child may arouse strong feelings within you and others because of his or her special needs and demands. As a human being, you, as the parent of a hearing-impaired child, experience all of the feelings other human beings experience. However, your feelings may be more intense as a result of the emotions you have involving your child's hearing impairment and the problems relating to your child's condition (Champ-Wilson, 1982). Also, you must remember that the grieving process described in chapter two is not a one-time experience. The grief associated with hearing impairment is special because its effects continue throughout your life and the life of your family. This chapter presents information about how feelings affect behavior. In other words, how you feel determines how you act. Being aware of your feelings as they occur will aid you in determining how best to act with your child as you meet challenging and new experiences in the future.

Skill Development

When you first learned about your child's disability you might have experienced a feeling that your world had come to an abrupt end. The hopes and dreams you had for yourself and your child vanished. Life is a series of adjustments. We are all continually faced with new challenges and new information. We eventually learn that when our world suddenly changes it is possible to rebuild a new one. In doing so, however, new goals and new expectations are made. Also, even though we may not wish to face one of life's givens, new pain and new frustrations will surface (Allen & Allen, 1979).

The feelings that you experienced at the moment you discovered you had a disabled child often recur. The grieving or mourning process is repetitive. Strong feelings such as severe anger or even subtle feelings such as mild sadness come into being when reality tells you that your child is different from others. Where an irreversible handicap is present in a child, the mourning process is open-ended. (Paget, 1983, p. 79). Throughout your child's life the disabling condition will present certain limitations on what he or she can do. At any stage of your life, you may experience some of the same feelings you had when you first discovered your child's disability. For instance, as your child

prepares for particularly important events, such as the first days of school, obtaining a driver's license, completing a job application, etc., the impact of your child's disability may again stir feelings of sadness, anger, or frustration within you.

When your feelings are not expressed, situations can become complicated and you may not recognize your true underlying feelings. For example, angry feelings you have about your child's disability can resurface. If you do not express or acknowledge this anger, you will be a prime candidate for the anger to be turned inward, and this can cause depression and guilt. It is only when you ignore your feelings that they may become troublesome. If you are aware that these feelings do occur, you can use them as a powerful coping resource. For example, once recognized, anger can be refocused away from the child and toward the disability. This can bring you closer to acceptance and help you start taking constructive action in adapting to new challenges and experiences.

It is important to remember that your feelings are a part of you but they need not take charge or control you. If you are not aware of your feelings or do not know what causes them, they can hinder your ability to make decisions. For instance, on a particular day your child may demand a lot from you. You may respond by arguing with your spouse when he or she arrives home. The argument stems from your not realizing the frustration you experienced earlier with your child. Your best action might be to discuss the situation and your frustrations with your spouse. Again, feelings that go unchecked are canceled and covered up by new thoughts. However, the feelings do remain and can continue to grow and become more bothersome.

> *It is important to remember that your feelings are a part of you but they need not take charge or control you.*

At times you and your family will be troubled regardless of the choices you make—whether it be how to handle a problem behavior or where to send your child to school. Never worry over whether you made the "one" right choice. There is never only one right decision. In making decisions, you should first express your feelings and then act on the information you have about your situation (Naiman & Schein, 1978).

In order to express your feelings you may need to do something active such as giving yourself time and permission to feel your feelings. Coping with your feelings may also involve shedding tears, taking a nap, or talking with a friend.

Applications

When a handicap is irreversible, the grieving process is open-ended. Hearing loss is an irreversible disability. From time to time you will be reminded that hearing loss impacts on your child's life and the lives of your family members. When your hearing-impaired child wants to play in the neighborhood, the reality of the hearing loss may bring forth feelings of concern about your child's safety, or fears that other children may treat your child badly. It is common to experience feelings such as fear, sorrow, and renewed grief when your child faces new challenges and new situations.

Being aware of your feelings can help you be more comfortable about your decisions. To illustrate this point, let's look at the example of your hearing-impaired child wanting to play in the neighborhood. Because of the disability, you may want to protect your child from harm or upset and want to keep him or her indoors. Parents *naturally* want to protect their children from pain, embarrassment, or harm. A parent's unresolved past feelings can, however, result in overprotection. You may feel guilty about the disability and feel sorry for your child. But overprotection helps only in the short run. In the long run, overprotection is harmful. It stifles your child's growth and presents an unrealistic picture of the world.

Hearing impairment should not obscure your view of your child. You do, however, need to understand the realistic limitations hearing impairment places on your child (Naiman & Schein, 1978). For example, hearing impairment places certain restrictions on your child's access to language development. Your child's hearing impairment will also limit the amount of information your child can receive since one channel (auditory) is disabled. Because your hearing-impaired child cannot receive the same verbal feedback about behavior, feelings, and thoughts provided to a normally hearing child, your child may not fully understand his or her experiences. Inevitably, other differences in behavior, emotional, and social development may be detected. Some of the social, emotional, and behavioral differences between hearing and hearing-impaired children will be detailed in chapter four.

As time goes on, strong feelings may influence and/or interfere with the way you manage your child's behavior. You may begin to wish that your child would be different or would be less of a burden. For example, your child, whom you loved as an infant, may be developing into a demanding, difficult person—a stranger with whom you cannot communicate. Also, each new developmental milestone, such as learning to read, may bring with it a return of old

When your hearing-impaired child wants to play in the neighborhood, the reality of the hearing loss may bring forth feelings of concern about your child's safety.

You and Your Hearing-Impaired Child

Overprotection helps only in the short run.

feelings and possibly troublesome new feelings. These experiences commonly occur in families of hearing-impaired children. The problems can be present regardless of the education or financial status of the family.

Feelings cannot be ignored. Each time you experience feelings you are also given the opportunity to learn. You may have to alter your family goals to adjust to your child's needs, and this may be unsettling to you and to your family. Remember, each of these new experiences brings growth. When there is growth, change occurs. When there is change, uncomfortable, difficult feelings or pain can occur as well. Experiencing pain provides the opportunity to develop strength for the future. The difficult feelings you experienced when your child was first diagnosed made you stronger and more prepared to deal with similar feelings in the future.

Keep in mind that many of the feelings you experience can and will be happy ones. You will be able to see the progress you and your child make. Feelings of sadness and sorrow can be replaced with happiness and excitement. When your child begins to communicate with other children and also with you, your heart will fill with joy. Share these feelings with special others. For these experiences proclaim the truth: Your child is a unique, loving, caring, and special person who happens to be hearing-impaired.

Your child is a unique, loving, caring, and special person who happens to be hearing-impaired.

Parent and Child

Unexpressed feelings interfere with your daily interactions with your child. Being a parent means you are in a position to make decisions. When you are aware of your feelings, your decisions are made more clearly. Listed below are statements from parents that reflect various levels of awareness of feelings. You can come to your own conclusions as to whether you believe their feelings will negatively or positively affect their actions. Following these examples is a list of guidelines that may help you cope with strong feelings and emotions.

"I try not to dwell on the hearing loss, my child is a great, good person who happens to be hearing-impaired."

"I am scared to discipline my hearing-impaired child like my hearing child; he has been through quite enough already."

"There's a lot of happiness out there and now we're going to find it!"

"For my own peace of mind, I've been upset and worried for a long time, I got my child an ID bracelet with her name, address, and phone number. Guess what—now all my children want one, too."

"I told my husband a joke. We laughed. My hearing-impaired son asked what I was laughing about. I felt so sad. I told him, 'Never mind.'"

"I know I'm angry at my child now for not looking at me when I'm explaining the situation. Now is not the time to punish him for this. I'm upset and he really doesn't know it."

"My hearing-impaired child closes his eyes when he wants to ignore me. I get so frustrated, I slap his hands."

"My child also closes his eyes to ignore me. I know that I get angry. I wait until he opens his eyes and gives me his attention. It takes a while, but by that time I have settled down as well."

Listed below are nine guidelines that you can use to deal with difficult feelings. These guidelines offer you ways to help you cope with your feelings. Books and other sources that may be useful in aiding you in dealing with feelings are found in the Suggested Reading section at the end of this book.

Coping with Your Feelings

1. Try to recognize the feelings you are experiencing. Make an attempt to name the feelings you are having. They are real and a part of you.

2. When your emotions are high, wait until they subside before you make major decisions. Many times strong emotions can get in the way of clear thinking.

3. Encourage members of your family and your friends to discuss their feelings honestly and openly. This can be done through your example.

4. Feelings are neither good nor bad. They are simply feelings. Always remember that everyone has feelings, but there is no one correct way to feel.

5. Talking to other people about the way you feel can help you cope. Feelings can become bottled up inside you. Sharing your feelings with others may help by relieving some of the tension you are experiencing.

6. Talking to other parents of hearing-impaired children will be helpful. These parents are experiencing or have experienced feelings and emotions similar to yours. Sharing with other parents of hearing-impaired children is important. You are not alone.

7. Gather information about hearing impairment from a variety of sources: other parents of hearing-impaired children, audiology centers, schools with services for the hearing impaired, books, service centers for hearing-impaired adults, etc. The more you know about hearing loss the more you can become aware of the realities of the hearing-impaired condition.

8. Continue the plans and routines you have set for you and your family. Discipline, family needs, family activities, etc. need to continue as usual. Your feelings may change from day to day, and hour to hour. Being aware of your feelings will help you control the impact they have on your life.

9. You are the best person to choose how to cope with your feelings. Physical exercise, prayer, reading, professional assistance, visiting friends, etc. are different ways people cope with their feelings. Choose or develop the best way that helps you cope.

The more you know about hearing loss the more you can become aware of the realities of the hearing-impaired condition.

Points to Remember

1. The grieving process is not a one-time experience. The grief associated with hearing impairment is special because its effects continue throughout your life and the life of your family.

2. An awareness of your feelings can assist you in being more comfortable about decisions.

3. When your feelings are not expressed, situations can become complicated and you may not recognize your true underlying feelings. If you do not express or acknowledge strong feelings, such as anger, you will be a prime candidate for these feelings to be turned inward, and this can cause depression and guilt.

4. Feelings such as anger can be refocused away from your child and toward the disability. This can bring you closer to acceptance and help you start taking constructive action in adapting to new challenges and experiences. Feelings can be used as a powerful coping resource.

5. Your feelings are a part of you but they need not take charge or control you.

6. In making decisions, you need to express your feelings and act on the information you have about your situation.

7. Your unresolved past feelings can result in overprotection. Overprotection helps only in the short run. In the long run, it is harmful because it stifles your child's growth and presents your child with an unrealistic picture of the world.

8. Feelings cannot be ignored. Each time you experience feelings you are also given the opportunity to learn, which is an opportunity to grow.

9. Many of the feelings you will experience can and will be happy ones. Share these feelings with special others. These experiences tell the truth: Your child is a caring, loving person who happens to be hearing-impaired.

1. In the previous chapter's activity, you wrote down ways to handle certain feelings that you experienced. We are now ready to go one step further. Examine some of what you do that eases your mind and helps you relax.

Physical exercise, prayer, reading, professional assistance, visiting friends, etc. are different ways that people cope with their feelings. Take a few minutes to write down several activities that calm your feelings and help you cope with a difficult situation.

Feeling	Coping Activity
_____	_____
_____	_____
_____	_____
_____	_____
_____	_____
_____	_____

Activities for Practice

These kinds of activities are ways of coping.

2. Take ten minutes to think about some of the ways hearing impairment affects your child's life and your life. What feelings are associated with these thoughts? Write these thoughts and feelings down. Also, if your feelings are strong ones, write down ways you and your spouse have used to handle these strong feelings.

Ways Hearing Impairment Has Affected You or Your Child's Life	Feelings This Brings About	Ways to Handle These Feelings
_____	_____	_____
_____	_____	_____
_____	_____	_____
_____	_____	_____
_____	_____	_____
_____	_____	_____
_____	_____	_____
_____	_____	_____

3. Take five minutes to think about how the discovery of hearing loss in your child has made you and other family members stronger or better. If you cannot think of any ways hearing loss has made you stronger, then consider ways it has changed your life. Write down your thoughts in the space below.

_____

_____

_____

_____

_____

_____

_____

_____

_____

_____

_____

_____

_____

4. One way to cope with feelings is to share them with someone who is understanding. Some parents of hearing-impaired children find it helpful to talk to other parents in a similar situation. If you have not done so already, think of another parent of a hearing-impaired child with whom you can talk. If you have given it some thought, write the name, address, and phone number of this person in the space provided.

Name of parent of hearing-impaired child:

_____

Address:

_____

_____

Telephone Number: (_____) _____

1. Read the sample problem below. Write down how you would handle this situation.

   You are out with your child at a nearby park. Several neighbors are also at this park. You let your child go to the swings where several other children are playing. These children begin to tease your child by laughing and pointing and saying, "Here's the Deafy."

   _____

   _____

   _____

   _____

   _____

   _____

   _____

2. True or False

   _____ a. Once you accept your child's hearing impairment you will no longer have to worry about feeling upset or sad, etc.

   _____ b. When you have troublesome feelings about your child being hearing-impaired, it is best to put these feelings and thoughts out of your mind because tomorrow you will feel better.

   _____ c. Unexpressed feelings can grow and become more complicated. They may make you feel worse as time goes on.

   _____ d. You need to be aware of the feelings that you have in order to get control of them and act constructively.

   _____ e. In the long run, it is better to protect a hearing-impaired child while he or she is young because he or she needs to know what limitations are caused by hearing impairment.

   _____ f. It is better to calm down if you are experiencing strong feelings before you make any major decisions.

   _____ g. It is better to ignore negative feelings and begin to think happy thoughts in order to go on doing something about your situation.

   _____ h. Activities such as physical exercise, prayer, reading books, going to the park, talking to others, etc. are all ways that help people cope with troublesome situations and feelings.

CHAPTER FOUR

Your Child's Behavior— What Is Normal?

INTRODUCTION

Growing up is a gradual process. Year by year your child will develop in many areas—social, emotional, cognitive, and physical. Your child's unique personality is heavily influenced by the learning that takes place each year. Yet this learning is but one factor that contributes to your child's personality and behavior. Other factors such as temperament, age, developmental rate, role, and position in the family also affect how your child behaves. Some youngsters are very active; others are very shy. Within the same family, children behave differently. Those of you who have several children can attest to this fact.

Parents are concerned about what is "normal" behavior. The word "normal" is hard to define. Each child responds as no other to differing situations. Furthermore, what may be a "normal" response by a child to one situation may not be acceptable in another situation. However, certain behavior patterns do exist at different ages. In other words, particular ways of behaving generally characterize children at certain ages. These are the result of emotional, psychological, and physical changes that occur at certain ages.

This chapter presents the typical behavioral growth patterns for children between the ages of two and ten. These ages represent critical developmental periods in a child's life that will affect all future behavior and personality development. Growth and development does not begin at age two and end at ten. The process continues from conception to death. However, ages two to ten are extremely important years affecting development of communication with others and with self (Heimgartner, 1982). Please note that the behaviors outlined are presented only as guidelines. Each child is unique. Your child may progress differently from the patterns outlined.

Skill Development

The previous two chapters dealt primarily with the feelings you experience in learning about your child's handicapping condition, and how these feelings recur as you react to the reality of the condition throughout your lifetime. Now let us move on to a discussion of child behavior.

This chapter discusses the always difficult and probably unanswerable question of what is "normal" behavior? A child's behavior and personality are affected by many factors in life. Physical characteristics with which a child is born, experiences throughout life, and how parents have raised the child are all influences on behavior and personality development. A handicapping condition is an additional influence on a child's behavior. For example, a child with a physical disability such as blindness or an educational disability that affects learning will have certain limitations placed on his or her world. These limitations have a direct impact on behavior. For instance, the blind child will be limited in areas requiring vision (e.g., reading written materials, recognizing familiar locations or surroundings, etc.). A mentally handicapped child may find it difficult to make choices among many alternatives. Finally, an emotionally handicapped child may strike another child due to his or her inability to control anger.

Because limitations determined by a disability will influence a child's behaviors and activities, determining what behavior is "normal" is more difficult. When behavior is influenced by a disability a parent must consider "normality" in light of the unique limitations placed upon the child due to the specific disability.

In order to make this special consideration, it is first important to review what behavior is more or less expected based on typical patterns of behavior found among children at the same age within the general population. This chapter will provide information to compare appropriate vs. inappropriate behavior at certain ages. A large portion of this chapter involves information about the different ages of a young child's life from the "terrible twos" to the "relaxed tens." Sit back, relax, and ready yourself for a journey focusing on the ways children typically behave at specific age levels. Some events and information presented on this journey will be very familiar; others may predict events yet to come.

This chapter involves a large amount of information, much of which may be of interest to you. You should, however, focus primarily on your child's age range. If time permits, you may want to read the information presented for each level.

The Two-Year-Old

This is a "run-about" age. Motor skills are unevenly developed. Two-year-olds are constantly active and curious about the world and about the environment (Peterson, 1982). Since children of this age are developing large muscle activity, they delight in rough-and-tumble play (Gesell, Ilg, & Bates-Ames, 1977). The energy of twos seems endless. They do not sit still for very long and are unable to last at any activity for a long period of time.

Curiosity is the hallmark of two-year-olds.

Curiosity is the hallmark of two-year-olds. They touch and taste everything because this is how they learn about their world (*Correspondence Course*, 1983). Two-year-olds are becoming more aware of the presence of others, yet, twos are unwilling to share their toys. A typical pattern is for them to cry and demand a toy, only to abandon it shortly for some new item or project.

Because two-year-olds are so active, much supervision is required. If wanted toys or activities are not provided, two-year-olds will seek out and discover their own experiences. This may lead to a knocked-over lamp or the banging of utensils on pans. Typically, these youngsters tend to be hesitant, defiant, ritualistic, unreasonable, and impulsive (Gesell et al., 1977).

The Three-Year-Old

Beginning with the third year of life, children become more conforming. Three-year-olds are less eager to take a room apart and more interested in order (*Correspondence Course*, 1983). They often enjoy putting things away in their proper places. They like to make choices. This is primarily due to the maturity of developing muscles. Three-year-olds have gained the physical ability to get around in their world. This period does not last for long, however. During the middle threes, the typical three-year-old appears to turn into a different person. Refusing to obey is perhaps the most notable personality characteristic. The simplest and smallest of occasions can bring forth total rebellion (Gesell et al., 1977).

Imagination continues to develop at this age, and it will play an important role in playtime activities. Insecure, anxious, and, above all, determined and strong-willed, best describe the child who is rounding out the third year of life (Gesell et al., 1977; Heimgartner, 1982).

Fours are very social.

The Four-Year-Old

The four-year-old may remind you of a more controlled two-year-old (*Correspondence Course*, 1983). Four-year-olds usually do everything for a purpose. Motor activity is advancing and is evidenced through a great deal of running, jumping, skipping, and climbing (Gesell et al., 1977).

Four-year-olds are becoming more assertive with their world and on occasion they are bossy. Four-year-olds are also becoming more imaginative, and they often exaggerate. Telling tall tales, bragging, and tattling are common. The four-year-old likes to be at center stage. Fours are very social and friends are becoming important. Playing outside the home is extremely beneficial for both muscular development and "showing off" learned skills.

Four-year-olds need to feel that they are important people. Praise and approval are needed at this age.

The Five-Year-Old

Fives are more friendly and in control of their environment (Brenner, 1983). Five is a self-contained age. Five-year-olds deal mainly with the here-and-now world even though it is complex.

Five-year-olds are realistic and concrete. They are ready to begin formal schooling—more eager to work than during the previous year. Their attention span has increased and they take pride in accomplishing tasks. Oftentimes five-year-olds have high expectations and frequently will take on more than they can handle.

Five-year-olds deal mainly with the here-and-now world.

Five-year-olds are developing control over their world. Because they are curious, they constantly ask questions. Five-year-olds are ready to take on small responsibilities, and although helpful, may become resistant and sensitive if over-taxed (Brenner, 1983; Gesell et al., 1977).

A five-year-old also begins to show a sense of humor. A surprise joke on mom and dad is not uncommon.

The Six-Year-Old

This age is characterized by a high level of activity. Six-year-olds learn best through active participation (Peterson, 1982). Six-year-olds are impulsive, active, excitable, and assertive (Gesell et al., 1977; Peterson, 1982). Since activity is sometimes described as the hallmark of six-year-olds, they also tire easily.

During this year of life, there are many inconsistencies in conduct. Six-year-olds often behave in extremes—a "love you/hate you" pattern. Remember that six-year-olds are experiencing changes in physical and psychological areas—for example, new teeth, and changes in the body's nervous system. Six-year-olds are also vulnerable to a whole range of infectious diseases (Gesell et al., 1977). Thus, parents must know that some conflict is inevitable and normal.

Six-year-olds thrive on the security of routines established in daily life. In other words, they enjoy the familiar. These children often have difficulty making decisions (Gesell et al, 1977; Heimgartner, 1982). They learn about the world mainly through imitation. Hence, they are highly dependent on directions and guidance from adults.

Parents are encouraged to praise good behavior whenever possible. It would be wise to teach this child appropriate and inappropriate behavior through the use of stories about other six-year-olds rather than by spanking or strong scolding (Gesell et al., 1977).

> *Six-year-olds learn best through active participation.*

The Seven-Year-Old

Seven-year-olds develop slowly and steadily. Sevens are good listeners and are interested in others' feelings and attitudes. Seven-year-olds can be described as inward, self-absorbed listeners.

Personality development is important at this age. Sevens may appear to brood a lot and become withdrawn. They often complain about events or people. The need for independence begins to surface. Therefore, parents must supply the right balance of independence and support. Remember, these children are still very dependent on reminders and adult guidance.

Behavior problems are not usually prevalent at this age. However, mood changes from calm and good to angry and tearful frequently occur. Lying and stealing may occasionally occur (Brenner, 1983). Remember that seven-year-olds are just beginning to develop ethically (Gesell et al., 1977). These new feelings and emotions are just beginning to take on meaning.

> *Parents must supply the right balance of independence and support.*

The Eight-Year-Old

Eight is an expansive age. Eight-year-olds show wide development in physical, social, and emotional areas (Gesell et al., 1977). Eight-year-olds are social and interested in others. These children are eager and enthusiastic. Activities involving explorations are common and eight-year-olds are very active indoors and outdoors. Eight-year-olds are evaluators of the events in their environment.

This is a social age. And, since eight-year-olds are very social, activity with peers becomes important. Most conflicts of this age involve peer interactions. Arguments and squabbles with friends are common.

This is also an age when the ethical sense is developing and maturing. Eight-year-olds display simple feelings of shame, and their feelings are easily hurt (Gesell et al., 1977).

Eight-year-olds, although far better self-controlled than younger children, still have difficulty grasping complex rules. Eight-year-olds are only beginning to draw conclusions and implications concerning the environment surrounding them.

Some behavior problems seen at this age stem from the eights' impatience. Eights often display slight tempers. They also can be overly dramatic and they have a tendency to be argumentative.

It is important for parents to be aware that eight-year-olds value a reward system (Gesell et al., 1977). Eights enjoy knowing when they have done well.

The Nine-Year-Old

Nine-year-olds are becoming more decisive, dependable, and fairly reasonable (Peterson, 1982). Several important psychological changes take place during this stage. Nines are developing self-motivation. Thus, they appear to have a reserve of energy to complete tasks again and again. Children of this age are not only able to continue on task for long periods of time, but they are also able to judge the job they have completed.

Along with certain changes in ability comes the development of new emotional patterns. For example, mood changes often occur. One day a nine-year-old is timid and cheerful; the next day this child is bold and grumpy (Gesell et al., 1977). In addition, the new emotional patterns often lead nine-year-olds to complain. Again, excessive complaining is most probably due to the growth process.

Nine is an age when strong feelings prevail. Nine-year-olds learn empathy—the ability to place themselves in another's shoes. Because of this new awareness and the development of other capabilities, nine-year-olds are better able to evaluate their decisions. It is not difficult to discipline nine-year-olds. Nine-year-olds can often be controlled merely by a look or a short isolation period from other children (Gesell et al., 1977).

The Ten-Year-Old

Ten-year-olds become more relaxed and content with themselves and with others. They are also more alert to both academic and social information.

The ten-year-old gives a fair indication of the person to be. Talents begin to surface and individual differences are readily apparent (Gesell et al., 1977). This is the age when the child's personality is significantly defined. Personality traits such as self-confidence are developing and strengthening. Parents are encouraged to reinforce the skills and talents of their ten-year-olds. Children of this age tend to have a strong sense of privacy. Secrets and private conversations with friends are common.

Ten-year-olds are entering "preadolescence." Preadolescence is a relatively new term in child development. Children in this phase are very different from children in the preschool and early school ages of two to ten. This age range is difficult to characterize because children

all behave differently as they react to the changes they undergo both physically and psychologically between the ages of nine and twelve. Children of this age range can present their parents with a variety of problems stemming from disrespectful behavior, need for approval from peer groups, sense of humor, and for some, the beginning of puberty. Preadolescents display bursts of energy coupled with a release of strong emotions. Preadolescents can appear angry, giddy, foolish, hilarious—but rarely are they calm.

Applications

A child goes through many psychological, emotional, and physical changes. Behavior is often a reaction to these changes. As the body grows and matures, behavior grows and matures. Each year of maturity brings forth characteristics unique to that year. The calmness of age five-and-a-half and the creativity of age six give way to the inward characteristics of seven, the expansiveness of eight, and the self-motivation of nine. Finally, there is the reorientation period of ten (Heimgartner, 1982).

A hearing-impaired child displays the same characteristics as those of a hearing child. The point to remember, however, is that the behaviors mentioned at each age are general characteristics but will not apply to all children. Each child is an individual, and individual differences determine the development of behavior. Many factors determine the way your child behaves, and hearing loss is one of those factors. Always keep in mind the total child. A hearing-impaired child is a person first—with all the physical, emotional, and intellectual needs that are characteristic of hearing peers.

You cannot ignore, however, the impact that the hearing-impaired condition will have on your child's behavior. The difficulties a hearing-impaired child experiences in language development will also be reflected through various ways in his or her behavior. Specifically, the delayed language development experienced by most hearing-impaired children leads to more limited social interaction and possible frustration (Meadow, 1980). One of the most frequently noted concerns regarding the social development of hearing-impaired children is that they seem to display a high degree of social and emotional immaturity (Bolton, 1976; Boothroyd, 1982; Liben, 1978; Meadow, 1980).

Many factors determine the way your child behaves, and hearing loss is one of those factors.

Social development and language are closely related. Delays in one area will most likely bring about delays in the other. Children with normal hearing begin to understand how their behavior affects other people through verbal interaction. They are told by their adult care givers or peers that their behavior is appropriate or inappropriate. Hearing-impaired children with little verbal language must rely more on facial expressions and gestures in trying to understand another's reactions to them. Interpretations based on these nonverbal communications may be less accurate, and this may lead to inappropriate responses from hearing-impaired children. For example, a hearing-impaired child does not hear a person's tone of voice, which indicates feeling or gives signals of wrongdoing, and therefore, may not know that he or she is about to break a limit placed on behavior. Hence, hearing-impaired children often have difficulty developing appropriate behaviors toward other people (Boothroyd, 1982).

A hearing-impaired child displays the same characteristics that all children do. However, these characteristics must be examined in light of the impact hearing loss has on behavior. Hearing-impaired children have been found to be less mature socially and emotionally. This is because difficulties in language influence social and emotional development. Since there is a delay in language for most hearing-impaired children, you can expect that they will lag behind what is expected as age-appropriate behavior at different levels throughout their lives. The behavior problems of hearing-impaired children seen by parents, teachers, and many professionals are likely tied to the expectations these adults have for hearing children at the same age (Meadow, 1980). It is extremely important for parents to view their hearing-impaired child's development in relation to the influence hearing loss has on behavior.

Since an inability to hear affects a child's language development, it will also affect the ability to communicate. Difficulty in communication will have an impact on a child's behavior. Limited communication may result in behavior that may seem inappropriate from time to time. A hearing-impaired child will have more problems expressing his or her wants and needs. The child may be more physical in his or her reactions to the environment. Since a hearing-impaired child's communication is more visual then auditory or vocal, the child is more likely to use visual and physical ways to communicate feelings, ideas, and thoughts. While hearing children may yell and scream to get their thoughts and emotions across, hearing-impaired children may gesture or even hit as well as vocalize their ideas and feelings (Deyo & Gelzer, 1987).

Let's examine a typical situation that might occur between a hearing-impaired child and a parent. The child wants to go outside because he sees a friend from the window playing in the yard at the house next door. The child points excitedly to go outside. The parent says no because it is nearing dinnertime. The child, not understanding why it is inconvenient for him to go outside, begins to cry and opens the door to leave. The parent, not knowing the reason for the child's persistence in leaving, communicates "No!" once again. The child slams the door, screams and yells, and runs to the bedroom. This behavior, seen by many as inappropriate, has developed from the misunderstanding of the communications sent by both parent and child. Frustration stemming from the inability to verbalize his wants and needs led to the child's physical and extreme behavior. This is only one example of how a child's behavior within a parent-child interaction can be influenced by the hearing impairment.

An individual's behavior, and ultimately an individuals personality, is shaped by what a person brings to his life (e.g., physical characteristics, experiences, etc.). A child's handicapping condition is as much a part of that child as are other characteristics such as eye color, height, body size, etc. The disability has an effect on a child's behavior and personality just like any other aspect of his or her life.

Reviewing what is generally expected from children at each age will give you a basis for judging your child's behavior as appropriate or inappropriate. Taking into consideration your child's hearing impairment will help you understand the reasons for your child's behavior. It is still important, however, to decide which behaviors should continue and which should be stopped. Using information from

> *A hearing-impaired child . . . is more likely to use visual and physical ways to communicate feelings, ideas, and thoughts.*

what you know about "normal" behavior and your knowledge of hearing impairment will help you make decisions about appropriate and inappropriate behaviors in your hearing-impaired child.

Some researchers have attempted to describe the typical behaviors of hearing-impaired children at particular ages. This information, though sparse, will be included in this section. The following descriptions will give you additional information from which to base your decisions on what is "normal" behavior for your hearing-impaired child.

The Hearing-Impaired Two-Year-Old

The use of gestures and/or manual communication may become an instrument of language because two-year-olds are able to express basic needs and wants (Heimgartner, 1982). However, the inability to communicate may lead to frustration, which is frequently released through temper tantrums (Brenner, 1983). Hearing-impaired children at this age through age five have been found to display temper tantrums much more often than hearing children (Gregory, 1976).

The Hearing-Impaired Three-Year-Old

Three is a good social age for children. Three-year-olds want to please both adults and peers. This is an age when fantasy is important. It is not uncommon for three-year-olds to talk, play-out, or sign with imaginary friends or pets. Such imaginary play and/or fantasy may be restricted somewhat due to the limitations placed on hearing-impaired children's language development (Meadow, 1980). For example, hearing-impaired children may need to pantomime or gesture a great deal more to convey an action or behavior that a single word could have expressed. The inability to communicate, however, does not prohibit fantasy and imaginary play (Heimgartner, 1982).

The Hearing-Impaired Four-Year-Old

Four-year-olds like to socialize. Four-year-olds also come to terms with their role in the family. Since these children are learning their role in the family, it is important to interact with them continuously. Letting four-year-olds share in structured routines and household activities is an important way for hearing-impaired children to understand their place in the family (Mindel & Vernon, 1987).

Parental love is extremely important to four-year-olds. You will be tested, however, with extremes of behavior. It is not uncommon to see your hearing-impaired child at one time saying, signing, or gesturing, "I hate you" and at another time saying, "I love you." Fits of laughter and then rage are common. Fours like to observe the reactions of adults (Heimgartner, 1982).

Letting four-year-olds share in structured routines and household activities is an important way for hearing-impaired children to understand their place in the family.

The Hearing-Impaired Five-Year-Old

Five is a curious age. Five-year-olds enjoy facts and information. Five is also the age when children are happy and content with the familiar. Hence, these youngsters enjoy a set routine at home (Heimgartner, 1982). Set routines help hearing-impaired children organize their

world. These structured periods of the day set expectations in their minds that help bring order to their lives. For five-year-old hearing-impaired children, structure and routine is vital to establish order and expectations.

Five-year-olds also stay at a task according to interest level, (e.g., may look at a picture book or work a puzzle for two minutes but play with friends for more than forty minutes).

The Hearing-Impaired Six-Year-Old

Six-year-olds abound with energy. They always seem to be running, jumping, and continually falling down. Sixes find it difficult to contain their energy and they often display impulsive and "excitable" behavior. This excess energy may at times affect hearing-impaired children's tolerance of situations where they are not understood. Frustration may build along with energy levels when they experience difficulties in communication. Six-year-olds often seem very noisy and loud. The loudness of the child's actions indicates the emotions stirring within (Heimgartner, 1982).

This age is typically an excitable and noisy one for all children, but hearing-impaired six-year-olds tend to have even louder and noisier interactions with their environment. The lack of feedback concerning sound will tend to lessen their ability to "tone down" the noise they make.

Remember that six-year-olds are learning to adjust to the demands of two environments—home and school. Within these environments there are interactions with both hearing and hearing-impaired children—possibly for the first time on a consistent basis.

The Hearing-Impaired Seven-Year-Old

Sevens are becoming more in control of themselves. Seven-year-olds never seem satisfied with their work. They appear to be perfectionists. This type of attitude carries on into their emotional development. Sevens are very sensitive, especially to the emotions and feelings of others. Seven-year-old hearing-impaired children are extremely sensitive to the expressions and body language of adults. Reading nonverbal language is important for these children in understanding about the thoughts and feelings of others.

Seven-year-old hearing-impaired children are extremely sensitive to the expressions and body language of adults.

The Hearing-Impaired Eight-Year-Old

Eight is an age when children are outgoing and argumentative. It is an extremely social age. It is an age when children recognize their hearing impairment and begin to accept it. Eight-year-old hearing-impaired children actively reach out to the hearing world for friendships (Heimgartner, 1982). To effectively communicate to peers and adults is a vital goal for youngsters of this age.

Eights are also very dramatic. Thus, signs, gestures, and verbalizations are all exaggerated. There is an increased awareness of the ability to pantomime and of its benefits in play and communication (Heimgartner, 1982).

The Hearing-Impaired Nine-Year-Old

Nine is a "settling down" age. Nine-year-olds exhibit control of emotions and of the environment. The child's personality is becoming apparent. Hearing impairment, communication style, sense of humor, etc. will all be more noticeable as unique to the child's personality.

At the same time, nine-year-olds are learning more and more about society. Nines are more aware of how individuals within society can behave toward one another. Nines are more aware of the prejudices of others (e.g., these children may get upset when excluded from games by hearing children). Nine-year-olds are impressionable, reasonable, and more independent (Heimgartner, 1982).

The Hearing-Impaired Ten-Year-Old

Many parents refer to this age as the golden age. Ten-year-olds have a matter-of-fact attitude. Parents need to explain and clearly define firm standards since ten-year-olds still need consistency and consequences. Ten-year-olds are able to make connections between events and their consequences. However, due to lags in language development, these connections need to be clearly explained and communicated in concrete terms. Clear communication of ideas and information is needed.

> *Parents need to explain and clearly define firm standards since ten-year-olds still need consistency and consequences.*

Parent and Child

This section contains some examples of typical statements that parents make about the behavior of their hearing-impaired children. These statements reflect thoughts and feelings certain parents have regarding their child's actions. Following each statement is a discussion concerning the appropriateness of the child's behavior considering the child's age and hearing impairment.

A mother of a two-year-old hearing-impaired child: "All my child ever does is throw temper tantrums—this is not normal and it frustrates me."

A two-year-old hearing child also displays temper tantrums on a regular basis, but hearing-impaired children tend to exhibit them more often because of their lack of communication abilities. It is important to note that tantrums can be expected of all two-year-olds.

A parent of a six-year-old hearing-impaired child: "I don't understand what has come over my Joey. He used to be so active. Now he is very withdrawn and seems fearful of adults."

A child this age is usually eager to learn and explore the environment. Although we must remember that each child is different and behaves in a unique way, if there is drastic change in behavior there may be a cause for concern.

A parent of a seven-year-old hearing-impaired child: "I do not know what is happening with Beth. She has been stealing money from her brothers and sisters. This must be because she is not getting enough of my attention. I will buy her more things."

> *Hearing-impaired children tend to exhibit tantrums more often because of their lack of communication abilities.*

This type of behavior from any child can be caused by many different reasons. It may be that the child is upset, or that (in this case) the child perceives that her sisters and brothers are the "winners" in the family. Thus, she feels the need to get back at them. Since this is the age when a child is maturing ethically, this behavior may also reflect the child's development in this area.

Remember that all behaviors have meaning and are communicators from your child. Even if a behavior is a part of normal development, you need to teach your child about appropriate and inappropriate behavior. The behavior characteristics of each age are only indications of what may be expected from your child. Parent management of those behaviors is still needed to help guide the child in developing a sense of self-control.

Points to Remember

1. Your child's unique personality is heavily influenced by the learning that takes place each year. But learning is just one factor that contributes to your child's personality and behavior. Temperament, age, developmental rate, role, and position in the family also affect how your child behaves.

2. Certain behavior patterns do exist at different ages. These are the result of emotional, psychological, and physical changes that occur at particular ages of a child's life.

3. The behavior patterns presented at each age are only guidelines. Every child is unique. Your child may progress differently from the pattern.

4. A child goes through many psychological, emotional, and physical changes. Behavior is often a reaction to these changes. A hearing-impaired child will display the same characteristics as those of a hearing child.

5. Many factors determine the way your child behaves. Hearing loss is one of those factors.

6. A hearing-impaired child is a person first—with all the physical, emotional, and intellectual needs of a hearing child. Do not let the hearing-impaired condition be the focus of your child's personality.

7. All behaviors have meaning and are forms of communication. But even if a behavior is characteristic of a certain age, it need not necessarily be tolerated. To develop a sense of self-control, children need to know what is appropriate and inappropriate behavior.

To develop a sense of self-control, children need to know what is appropriate and inappropriate behavior.

Do this activity one step at a time—a, b, and then c.

1. a. During the next two days, take ten minutes toward the end of each day to write down the type of day your hearing-impaired child has had. Specify behaviors you have noticed throughout the day.

_____

_____

Day One
(Date:)

_____

_____

_____

_____

_____

_____

_____

_____

_____

_____

_____

_____

Day Two
(Date:)

_____

_____

_____

_____

_____

_____

_____

_____

_____

Activities for Practice

b. Check over the behaviors that you have listed in *a.* and mark down whether you consider these behaviors to be "normal" and age-appropriate or inappropriate for your child's age.

Behavior	Age-appropriate	Age-inappropriate
_____	_____	_____
_____	_____	_____
_____	_____	_____
_____	_____	_____
_____	_____	_____

c. Compare the comments that you made about your child's behavior with the descriptions listed under your child's age in the Skill Development and Applications sections. Are your views of your child's "normal" or age-appropriate behavior accurate? Are your views of your child's age-inappropriate behavior accurate?

Write your comments here

_____
_____
_____
_____
_____

2. Look at the observations of your child's behavior you listed in the previous activity. Try to recall whether these behaviors have appeared in previous months or are new behaviors. Using this additional information, again decide on whether the behavior is age-appropriate for your child or age-inappropriate.

Write your comments here

_____
_____
_____
_____
_____

1. Read the sample problem below. What do you think of this situation? Knowing what you know about the child's age and behavior, what do you think about this child's behavior?

   A four-year-old hearing-impaired child wants to buy a toy at the grocery store. The parent says, "No!" The child throws himself on the floor and screams and cries and will not leave the store unless carried.

   _____

   _____

   _____

   _____

   _____

   _____

   _____

   _____

2. True or False

   _____ a. A child's personality and behavior is affected by age, developmental rate, position in the family, and the learning that takes place every day.

   _____ b. Behavior patterns do exist for children at certain ages and these patterns should be used to determine whether a child's specific behaviors are normal or abnormal.

   _____ c. All children progress through different stages and behavior patterns at the same rate.

   _____ d. The behavior patterns listed in this chapter are general guidelines about children's behavior and should not be used as specific examples of "normal" behavior.

   _____ e. A two-year-old who displays temper tantrums should be observed carefully. Temper tantrums are unusual for children of this age.

   _____ f. A ten-year-old is going through tremendous changes in growth. This child is hard to manage and discipline.

   _____ g. A hearing-impaired child displays the same characteristics and needs as a hearing child because of growth and development.

   _____ h. Hearing loss is only one of the factors that determines how your child behaves.

CHAPTER FIVE

Setting Limits

INTRODUCTION

All human beings must learn restraint—how to limit their own behavior. Some things come naturally. Physically, children mature naturally. They progress from lying down to sitting, standing, and finally walking. This process of physical maturation requires very little help from parents (Brenner, 1983). But other aspects of growing require direction and training from parents. As seen in chapter four, children behave differently throughout the growing process. Much of a child's behavior is learned (Kazdin, 1984). Children need to learn the basic limits of their behavior. Depriving them of learning limits leaves them without the coping skills and possibly the opportunity to develop self-control. This leaves them helpless in a society that demands conformity to rules and regulations.

We often describe the process of setting limits on behavior as discipline. Appropriate behavior must be taught just like other behaviors. It is important for anyone who is involved with disciplining children to structure what children are to be taught. Your adult world was not designed with your child in mind. You are comfortable in the adult world because you know that much of what comes your way is more or less expected (Baker, Brightman, Heifetz, & Murphy, 1976). Limits provide expectations for children and aid them in making their world a bit more manageable.

Skill Development

Children progress in their physical, emotional, and psychological capabilities through their lifetime. Children also progress with respect to their self-control—learning what is appropriate and inappropriate behavior as they pass through certain ages. Although different behaviors are characteristic of particular ages, children still must know how to limit their behavior and develop a sense of self-control.

Learning self-control is much like developing any new skill. Uncontrolled behavior may be disappointing or even irritating to others in the environment. Children need guidance and limits in order to develop the skill of self-control so that they will be accepted in the world in which they live. Setting limits is necessary to provide for a child's safety and well-being. Limits also help the child to develop a consideration for others (*Correspondence Course,* 1983). Do not feel guilty about having to set limits for your child's behavior. When you set limits, you establish a secure atmosphere where learning can take place.

When you set limits, you establish a secure atmosphere where learning can take place.

Most aspects of growing up require training. In this sense, a parent is a teacher. There is no magic formula for determining how to set limits. However, some structure or plan is necessary to teach your children what you want them to learn. To teach children about appropriate and inappropriate behaviors, you need to be very clear about limits. An important rule of thumb is that *you must be consistent in applying rules or limits*. For example, if you decide there are certain boundaries for outside play, be clear about why it is important to have such boundaries. And then be consistent about your decision.

You convey rules and limits about behavior to your children mostly through example (Ogden & Lipsett, 1982). You also teach limits through developing routines. Most children like and prefer routines that structure their day. Hence, you need to structure mealtime, clean-up time, and bedtime so your child can develop and expect routines. This will bring order to your child's life. Remember that people act differently in different situations. People act differently at home, in school, at church, at a football game, in business meetings, driving a car, giving a speech, listening to music, or while eating dinner. Being specific about your limits is important (Madsen & Madsen, 1972). You must work with specific situations when teaching proper limits so that your child will know what your expectations are in a particular situation. Only you can decide what is appropriate for your child.

Let us look at a specific example about setting limits. You decide there will be no watching of television until after dinner. So in the late afternoon and during dinnertime in your home, between the hours of 3:30 P.M. to 6:00 P.M., the television remains off. Now, there can be several reasons for your decision. Perhaps this is a good time for your child to complete homework, to rest after a busy day, or to play out side to release energy. For whatever reason, you decide to set this limit.

> *When you set limits, it is important to state the imposed limits in a positive form.*

When you set limits, it is important to state the imposed limits in a positive form. It is natural for adults to use the word, "no." Your child expects to hear it. In fact, it is one of the first words a child speaks. "No" is a powerful word meaning, "bad," "stop," or other negative things. When setting limits, however, this word is almost useless. To a younger child it commonly means the activity is bad. To an older child the "no" is interpreted as an order instead of a reasonable limit to behavior. The most important reason for avoiding the word "no" is that it tells the child what not to do, but does not tell the child what he or she may do. Therefore, it is advisable to state all limits in the positive. For example, instead of your limit being "No television watching from 3:30 P.M. to 6:00 P.M.," it may be "Television can be watched after 6:00 P.M. only."

Other examples follow:

Negative	Positive
1. No fighting with neighborhood children.	1. Only nice play with other children.
2. No swearing.	2. Use polite language.
3. No yelling and screaming in the house.	3. Talk quietly and softly, or use a nice voice in the house.

Stating your rules in a positive manner is the first step to providing clear limits to your child's behavior.

Rewards are important for letting your child know your rules have been followed and that he or she has acted appropriately. You can establish your own reward system using praise, hugs, extra play time, etc., for maintaining the limits in your household. In other words, whenever your children are doing what you wish—let them know it!

You may wonder what to do when your child breaks your rules. Should you send your child to his or her room? Should you take away TV privileges? Do not wait until your child misbehaves to develop your limits. The more prepared you are, the easier it will be to help your child stop the misbehavior. Whenever possible, the action you take after the behavior (called consequences) should be logically related to the behavior (Canter & Canter, 1985; Dinkmeyer & McKay, 1976).

You will more quickly teach your children appropriate behavior when the consequences you use logically relate to the misbehavior.

For example:

Misbehavior	Logical Consequence
1. Your nine-year-old breaks your kitchen appliance.	1. Child is not allowed to use your appliances for one week.
2. Your seven-year-old willfully breaks your three-year-old's favorite toy.	2. Child must use own allowance to buy another toy.
3. Your four-year-old uses a crayon to color the living room walls.	3. Child is required to clean the living room walls.

> *A child needs to test limits in order to explore, discover, and learn.*

Each consequence must have a direct connection to the misbehavior. There are other points that you must remember when your child chooses to misbehave. First, whenever your child misbehaves, he or she should be given a choice to follow your limit. For example, "Scott, I cannot allow you to poke and hit your brother while playing. If you hit your brother again you will choose to sit and be in your room alone with no toys." You have now provided your child with a choice. If your child decides to continue to hit or poke, you simply say, "Scott, you hit your brother. You have chosen to go to your room." When you give your child choices, you provide him or her with the opportunity to learn the natural consequences of his or her behavior. Your child also learns to be responsible for his or her actions (Canter & Canter, 1985). In order to be consistent with your application of consequences, the consequences must follow *every* time the child chooses to misbehave.

Second, remember that children will test limits. Some children will test them continuously. This is normal. A child needs to test limits in order to explore, discover, and learn (*Correspondence Course*, 1983). This process helps your child to develop expectations about his or her world. Child management, frequently called "discipline," is the means by which a child learns. Discipline is the procedure used to guide a child through safe and healthy channels (*Correspondence Course*, 1983).

You can begin to discipline your child by setting fair and consistent limits.

Applications

All children need to learn restraint and control. Hearing-impaired children are no exception. In order to teach hearing-impaired children limits and restraints, you need to consider the hearing impairment. Hearing-impaired children have the same needs as hearing children. They need to feel secure, loved, and important. The need for a healthy family environment, one which is physically and psychologically safe, is no different for a hearing-impaired child. Parents of hearing and hearing-impaired children alike must explain the world to their offspring. However, parents of hearing-impaired children need to provide more explicit explanations (Mindel & Vernon, 1987; Ogden & Lipsett, 1982). This means that *what you teach your child must be clearly demonstrated*. Your child must clearly understand what is expected in specific situations. You must communicate limits to your child.

Your hearing-impaired child has unique communication needs. Due to the hearing disability, you may be concerned about how to define expectations, limitations, and boundaries to your child. The relation of discipline to communication is a close one. Discipline itself is a communication process. This process relies on the language you use to convey your thoughts, feelings, and ideas to your child.

Early development of an effective language system will help you discipline your child. Many people view language as only involving the production of speech. But language involves both verbal and nonverbal means of communication. A narrow definition of language is particularly confining when discusssing language and the hearing-impaired child. Since your child's hearing is impaired, it is important to capitalize on other channels of communication. The child uses channels such as vision, hearing (residual), touch, distance, vocalizations, facial expressions, and body movements as avenues of communication (Proctor, 1983). You can use these channels of communication to develop an effective language system with your child.

Remember that a child who does not receive incoming messages through the auditory channel must depend on input through the other channels (physical contact, facial expressions, etc.) to receive feedback about his or her world. Therefore, being competent in the use of language with your hearing-impaired child does not mean the use of oral language only, but any means that can be used to aid you in helping your child to understand himself or herself and others (Mindel & Vernon, 1987).

Developing effective language is related to the availability of life experiences. Language structures reality for your child and permits him or her to organize experiences in order to understand and control his or her environment (Boothroyd, 1982). A child learns meaning first and then words. For example, a child can learn the meaning of *hot* if you put the child's hand in hot water. The word *hot* is learned by connecting the word to the experience (i.e., the meaning). The important people in the child's life must help provide this meaning.

Everything a hearing-impaired child must learn, whether it be boundaries of playing outside or appropriate behaviors allowed before dinner, must be taught explicitly. Remember that most hearing children pick up acceptable behavior through imitation and from auditory cues. Hearing-impaired children must be explicitly told and

---

Early development of an effective language system will help you discipline your child.

Everything a hearing-impaired child must learn, ... must be taught explicitly.

You and Your Hearing-Impaired Child

shown how to act. A hearing-impaired child must be taught through the use of nonverbal means of communication as well as verbal. Your child must be shown meaning through photographs, drawings, demonstrations, and modeling to develop an understanding of the boundaries and limits of the world. For example, you can show your child what appropriate behavior is expected by demonstrating proper behavior in the play area (handling toys gently, using crayons only with paper, etc.), and you can also illustrate proper behavior or limits on behavior by drawing pictures.

For example:

You can show your child what appropriate behavior is expected by demonstrating proper behavior ... and ... by drawing pictures.

Communicating limits to a hearing-impaired child is not easy. But parents who are successful give clear guidelines and limits to their children. And these parents believe the extra effort is worthwhile. Keep in mind that children will test even learned limits. A child with expressive language will verbally test the limits while a child without verbal language will test more concretely (through physical contact, a spilled dish, etc.) and may give the impression of being less well behaved (Boothroyd, 1982). A hearing-impaired child needs to test limits in order to discover and understand the world and give meaning to it. Teaching your hearing-impaired child limits is difficult. You must provide more explanations for your child by example, drawings, gestures, signing, or whatever method you believe is effective. This probably means that your task is to develop a better sense of your child's environment by being more attentive to it.

Parent and Child

The following situations illustrate limit setting by parents of hearing-impaired children. Review the parents' use of rules, explanations, and consequences when setting limits for their children. Remember that each rule should be stated in the positive and the consequence should be logically related to the misbehavior.

A nine-year-old hearing-impaired child loves to paint pictures. The child enjoys painting in the family room with members of the family present. The child's father sets the following limit:

Limit
Use proper care while painting (specifically, lay down papers, keep paint brushes in container, etc.).

How limit is explained
Parent draws a picture of a neat painting area—brushes are shown in container, all sheets of trash are placed in trash can, etc. He also draws a picture of his child, smiling, within the area.

If limit is broken: Consequence
Child will paint in basement during the next play session.
or
Child will not be allowed to use paints during next play session.

A twelve-year-old hearing-impaired boy wishes to stay awake an extra hour (until 10:00 P.M.) during weekend evenings. His parents decide to make the following rule:

Limit
Child must be in bed by 10:10 P.M.

How limit is explained
Parents demonstrate through examples that the child must be in bed by 10:10 each evening. Using a portable clock with a large face, the parents point to the clock at 10:00 P.M. Child is then shown that he must wash, brush his teeth, change his clothes, and be in bed by 10:10 P.M. The parents point to the clock again showing the time limit.

If limit is broken: Consequence
Minutes will be deducted from next evening's time limit. For example: If the child is five minutes late (gets in bed at 10:15 P.M.), he goes to bed five minutes earlier the next evening (must be in bed by 10:05 P.M.).

A four-year-old hearing-impaired girl wishes to play with a friend in the backyard. However, she has difficulty sharing. She gets angry when other children want to play with her toys. The child's parents develop the following limit:

Limit
Nice play only in the backyard.

How limit is explained
Mother and father model good sharing and playing behavior for the child. The child is shown how two people can enjoy playing together. Also, the child is shown proper ways to play with toys and ways to share with other children. The four-year-old is also praised with words, smiles, and hugs when sharing and playing appropriately.

If limit is broken: Consequence
Child will play alone the next time she plays in the backyard. She is not allowed to play with the toys she would not share.
or
Child is kept inside during the next playtime.

Points to Remember

1. Physically, children mature naturally—they progress from lying down to sitting, standing, and then to walking. This process occurs with little help from parents. However, other aspects of growing require direction and training from parents. Children need to learn the limits of their behavior.

2. We often describe the process of setting limits on behavior as discipline. Appropriate behavior, like other behaviors, must be taught.

3. You must set limits to provide for a child's safety and well-being, and to help your child develop consideration for others. Do not feel guilty about having to set limits for your child's behavior.

4. You must develop a structure or plan to teach your child what you want him or her to learn. To teach your child about appropriate behavior, you must be very clear about limitations.

5. You must be consistent in applying rules or limits.

6. A child will test limits in order to learn or discover about his or her world.

7. People act differently in different situations. We act differently at church, in school, when listening to music, in business meetings, while eating dinner, etc. Being specific about your limits is important.

8. All children need to learn restraint and control. Hearing-impaired children are no exception.

9. Parents of hearing and hearing-impaired children alike must explain the world to their offspring. Parents of hearing-impaired children, however, need to provide more explicit explanations.

10. A hearing-impaired child needs to test limits in order to discover and understand the world and give meaning to it. Teaching your hearing-impaired child limits is not easy.

1. We act differently in different settings. List three specific situations your child is continually involved in. Examples include sitting at the dinner table or playing in the play area. Now decide on two limits that you would place on your child's behavior and list these for each specific situation noted.

Example:

Situation
Sitting at the dinner table.

Limits
1. Being seated is necessary at all times.
2. Use polite table manners.

Be sure to state limits in the positive.

Situation

_____

_____

_____

_____

_____

Limits

1. _____

_____

_____

2. _____

_____

_____

Situation

_____

_____

_____

_____

_____

Limits

1. _____

_____

_____

2. _____

_____

_____

Situation

_____

_____

_____

_____

_____

Limits

1. _____

_____

_____

2. _____

_____

_____

2. Using the information you provided for activity 1, decide how you can best explain these limits to your child. In what ways would you clearly convey these rules to your child? Develop these thoughts further by explaining details about how you would or do convey the limits you set.

_____

_____

_____

_____

_____

_____

_____

_____

3. Review the six limits you have listed in the above activities. Are these limits important in the long run? Yes ___ No ___ . If they are, take three of the limits listed and decide on the consequence you would place on the child if each limit is broken. Try to connect the consequence logically to the misbehavior.

Example:

Limit	Consequence of Breaking Limit
1. Only careful play with toys permitted.	1. Child cannot play with toys for one day. or 2. Child must replace toy with his or her own money.

Limit	Consequence of Breaking Limit
_____	1. _____ _____
_____	2. _____ _____
_____	3. _____ _____

1. Read the sample problem below. Given what you know about limit setting, what steps would you take to limit your daughter's behavior? How would you handle this situation?

   Your ten-year-old hearing-impaired daughter has difficulty doing her chores around the house. She does her work sometimes and other times does not. She tells you she is tired, or that she wants to meet her friends, or she must work on her schoolwork.

   _____

   _____

   _____

   _____

   _____

   _____

   _____

   _____

2. True or False

   _____ a. Setting limits can be described as discipline.

   _____ b. Children will develop self-control on their own as they mature; there is no need to set limits to their behavior as they get older.

   _____ c. Limits must be applied consistently.

   _____ d. Setting general limits to behavior is more important than being specific about them. Children will be confused as to what is appropriate and not appropriate if your limits are too specific.

   _____ e. It is beneficial to state limits in a positive form because they tell the child what behavior is appropriate.

   _____ f. Whenever possible, the consequence you place on the child after misbehavior should be logically connected to that misbehavior.

   _____ g. Limits should be explained to hearing and hearing-impaired children in the same manner. It is not necessary to do any more for a hearing-impaired child.

   _____ h. Limits can be shown and explained to a hearing-impaired child through the use of drawings, gestures, voice, signing, or any method you believe to be effective as long as the limits are clearly explained.

CHAPTER SIX

The A-B-C's of Behavior Management

INTRODUCTION

All parents are concerned about their children's behavior. Parents who establish clear limits and consistently enforce those limits have made the first step in structuring their offspring's world so that learning can take place. Chapter five discussed the importance of setting limits and how to follow through when children test these limits. General guidelines and basic principles were given for limit setting (the fundamental groundwork for the day-to-day practice of discipline). Sometimes, however, you may find that your child continually displays problem behavior or that a specific problem behavior needs special attention. Such problem behaviors may interfere with how effectively your child learns appropriate behavior. These problem behaviors can be disruptive to those who interact with your child. Chapter six will help you deal with these special problem behaviors.

Individuals who work or live with a child must decide if a particular behavior truly is a problem. In order to do this, you must examine the behavior according to its intensity (strength), frequency (how often it occurs), age appropriateness, and how it affects you. Once you decide that your child is exhibiting a "problem behavior," you must develop a plan for helping your child control this behavior. A plan will also help you develop opportunities for your child to practice appropriate behaviors and replace problem ones.

This chapter will help you reduce the occurrence of problem behaviors in your child and enhance your knowledge of effective behavior management practices.

> *Remember that all parents are in the business of changing, modifying, or limiting their children's behavior.*

Skill Development

Before developing a plan for managing your child's specific behaviors, you must first decide whether the behavior in question is actually a problem. Some obvious problem behaviors are tantrums, biting, fighting, and refusing to obey. Other less obvious problem behaviors include not paying attention, crying, and making annoying noises. All children are capable of displaying annoying behaviors that prove troublesome or stressful to parents. You must decide the behaviors you want to limit and change. Remember that all parents are in the business of changing, modifying, or limiting their children's behavior. What determines success is whether you use a plan to change behavior.

After you have identified your child's behavior as a problem you are ready to use a strategy to change it. Behavior modification is one effective way to do so.

The behavior-modification approach is based on important principles that help change unwanted behaviors in children. The principles of this method are these: (1) Your child will tend to repeat a behavior that brings a pleasurable or good outcome. (2) Your child will avoid behaviors that do not produce a favorable outcome. This is a scientific approach. This approach will help you change your child's behavior by helping you understand the purpose and reason for the behavior.

Systematic use of the behavior-modification approach will give purpose and direction to methods you have probably used for a long time. If you consistently follow the plan, you will achieve the desired results. The most difficult part is consistency. But following a plan helps make what you do clear to you and your child. And a plan aids in making your actions consistent. The A-B-C framework is such a plan.

The A-B-C Plan

Before changing a child's behavior, you must first carefully observe that behavior to understand it and see more clearly what needs to be changed. In order to change behavior, you will need three pieces of information:

1. The setting in which the behavior takes place (antecedents);

2. The specific behavior that occurs (behavior);

3. The actions that follow in that particular setting (consequences) (Baker et al., 1976).

If you know the setting in which the behavior occurs, the behavior, and the actions that follow the behavior, you will more clearly understand if the behavior will continue. Again, remember this simple rule: "Behavior that is followed by something pleasant is likely to happen again" (Baker et al., 1976; Herbert, 1981).

You must view the behavior you want to change within the context in which it occurs. This is necessary because the same behavior occurring in different contexts is handled differently. For example, you handle a child crying when there are no lights on in a room differently from a child crying because of a dog bite.

Antecedents

Behavior is what you first see when observing your child. First, you must decide whether your child is displaying a "problem behavior." If you decide he or she is, it is time to observe the behavior in detail. To change a behavior, you must know what you want to change. You need to clearly identify the behavior that you see. As an agent of behavior change, you must learn to specify, in exact terms, the problem behavior (Baker et al., 1976; Kazdin, 1984). For example, a mother might complain that her eight-year-old boy is fussy before dinner every evening. "Fussy" is a general term that could mean different things to different people. Further discussion might reveal that the mother actually means the child cries when asked to come to dinner. "Cries before he comes to the dinner table" is a specific behavior that can be easily observed by others. Specifying the behavior is the first step to developing a plan for behavior change. Words like "acting aggressive," "stubborn," or "fussy," are not specific; they do not pinpoint the child's problem behavior.

Behavior

Consequences are the actions that follow a behavior. Quite often the consequences determine whether a behavior will happen again and how often. Consequences include actions such as approval (rewards), disapproval (punishment), ignoring, or threats. Some rewards are praise, money, enjoyment, and candy. Some punishments are taking something away that a child likes, scolding, and spanking.

Consequences

There are no universal rewards or punishments. Every child is different. Your job is to discover the most effective rewards and punishments for your child. How effective a given consequence is in a situation with a given behavior can be determined only by each child's experience. In other words, through your interactions with your child, you will discover which consequences work and which do not.

The foundation of behavior management is consistency. The A-B-C pattern is a framework that provides guidelines for consistency. Read the following examples of the A-B-C pattern and examine each part of the pattern to determine if the example fits with what you know about the A-B-C's of behavior.

A Antecedent	B Behavior	C Consequences
Before dinner, Mom and Dad are preparing dinner and are talking. Joey gets no attention.	Joey cries before dinner.	Mom and Dad stop what they are doing and go see what is wrong. Joey gets attention.
Grandma arrives for a visit.	Sally runs up and gives Grandma a kiss.	Grandma gives Sally a dollar bill.
Dad asks Julie to do the dishes before she goes out with her friend.	Julie goes out without doing the dishes.	Julie is grounded and is not allowed to go out with her friend for one week.

Can you predict what will happen in the future for each case? Use the principles of behavior modification to make your prediction. Remember: Behavior that is followed by a pleasant outcome is likely to happen again. Behavior that is not followed by something pleasant or rewarding will be avoided.

Joey's behavior is likely to happen again because Joey received a positive outcome (attention) from his behavior (crying). Sally's behavior of affection to her grandmother will also likely happen again because of her grandmother's rewarding response. On the other hand, Julie's disobedience may stop because of the negative consequence of her actions.

Applications

When trying to understand behavior, remember that no two children are alike—each child is unique. Behavior is the way your child tells you what he or she needs or desires. Hearing impairment limits the opportunities for expressing needs. Hearing impairment does not make your child different; it adds to the child's uniqueness.

You need a consistent framework to change your child's behavior. You can obtain consistency by keeping your child's daily routines as stable as possible. Let your child know his or her part in the overall plan of management within the home. Structure in your home will help your child develop expectations about the world. Setting limits will also help your child develop these expectations.

The A-B-C pattern can provide a consistent framework to help you apply limits. Again, remember that your child will repeat any behavior that brings good outcomes. Hearing-impaired children have the same needs as hearing children. In applying a set of rules to hearing-impaired children, you must remember that communicating ideas—getting your points across—will take extra time. This is the reality of hearing impairment. *Ideas and issues taken for granted in*

> *Behavior that is followed by a pleasant outcome is likely to happen again.*

raising a hearing child must be made explicit for a hearing-impaired child (Mindel & Vernon, 1987; Ogden & Lipsett, 1982). The A-B-C pattern offers a framework for establishing consistency and for making explicit the rules necessary to change the behavior of your hearing-impaired child.

Hearing impairment has little negative effect on the success of behavior-management techniques such as the A-B-C pattern (Algozzine, Schmidt, & Mercer, 1981; Belcastro, 1979; Mira, 1972). However, you do need to be more careful in pinpointing which behaviors are problems and which are not. Sometimes what may appear to be a behavior problem is only an attempt to communicate. For example, your child may continually tap or hit you, while speaking to you, to gain your attention. You can correct this behavior by looking at your child when he or she is talking. Otherwise, your child may fear that you have missed something. Careful observation of the behavior (specifying exact behavior) within the setting in which the behavior occurs (antecedents) and noting what happens after the behavior occurs (consequences) can help you pinpoint the severity of the behavior problem and what helps it continue.

The A-B-C pattern is mainly used to develop consistency so a behavior problem can be changed. This pattern is particularly effective with hearing-impaired children because it does not rely on language for its success (Mira, 1972). The following example illustrates how a mother of a hearing-impaired seven-year-old child can use the A-B-C pattern to identify a problem behavior.

A Antecedent	B Behavior	C Consequences
Child grabs item wanted (food, toy, etc.). Mother pulls it away. She communicates, "No!"	Child cries, whines, stamps foot. Temper tantrum occurs.	Mother gives item to child to stop problem behavior.

This child's behavior is highly inappropriate for a seven-year-old. Identifying the behavior is part of the modification process. Using the A-B-C pattern, the parent can examine the setting in which the tantrum behavior occurs, and what happens following the behavior. After identifying the antecedents and/or consequences that help the behavior continue, this mother can determine how best to alter the pattern to stop or decrease the misbehavior and create the desired behavior. Techniques for altering the A-B-C pattern to change behavior will be presented in chapter seven.

Parent and Child

The following stories illustrate certain problem behaviors shown by hearing-impaired children. Analyze each situation. See if your analysis matches the A-B-C pattern given.

"Charlie is really driving us crazy. Every time he plays with neighborhood children, he bites them. We are afraid that soon he will have no one to play with."

A Antecedent	B Behavior	C Consequences
Charlie and neighbor child are playing with toys. Charlie wants toy from other child. Child refuses.	Charlie bites child.	Other child cries. Gives Charlie toy. Runs home to tell parents about toy and bite.

"I'm so frustrated with Sam. When I work with him using language blocks, he yells and makes horrible noises. The class is disrupted too much. I allow him to use the color board until he calms down."

A Antecedent	B Behavior	C Consequences
Teacher brings language blocks to Sam. Sam hates working on language skills.	Sam screams, yells, and makes noises.	Teacher gives Sam the color board to calm down. He is able to avoid working on language. He likes to color.

"Joanie is now so much better when going to bed. I told her I would read her one story each night as long as she is dressed and in bed by nine o'clock. Boy, she loves stories."

A Antecedent	B Behavior	C Consequences
Mother reminds Joanie to be in bed by nine o'clock, ready for the story.	Joanie gets ready for bed and is in bed by nine o'clock.	Mother comes into the room and sees Joanie in bed. She reads one of Joanie's favorite stories.

Points to Remember

1. Limit setting provides the fundamental groundwork for the day-to-day management of behavior. Sometimes you may find that your child continually displays problem behavior or that a specific problem behavior needs special attention.

2. All children are capable of displaying annoying behaviors that prove troublesome or stressful to parents. You must decide which behaviors you want to limit and change.

3. All parents try to change, modify, or limit their children's behavior. What determines success is whether you use a plan to change behavior.

4. The behavior-modification approach is based on important principles that help change unwanted behaviors in children.

5. The principles of behavior modification are that (1) Your child will tend to repeat a behavior that brings a pleasurable or good outcome. (2) Your child will avoid behaviors that do not produce a favorable outcome.

6. The most difficult aspect of changing behavior is consistency. Following a plan helps make what you do clear to you and your child.

7. The A-B-C pattern provides a framework for consistency:

    (A) Antecedents: the setting in which the behavior takes place;

    (B) Behavior: the specific behavior that occurs;

    (C) Consequences: the actions that follow the behavior in that particular setting.

8. No two children behave alike. Each child is unique. Hearing impairment does not make your child different, it adds to his or her uniqueness.

9. Hearing impairment has little negative effect on the success of the A-B-C pattern. In fact, this pattern is particularly effective with hearing-impaired children because it does not rely on language for its success.

1. Take ten minutes to describe an interaction you have had with your child that involved a misbehavior. Describe your child's specific behavior and how you responded to that behavior. Finally, describe how your child reacted to your response. How do you feel about the interaction? Was your response effective?

Your Child's Behavior	Your Response	Your Child's Reaction

2. If you are not satisfied with the outcome of the interaction described in activity 1, analyze this interaction using the A-B-C pattern. If you are satisfied with the outcome of the interaction, then choose another interaction involving misbehavior that you would like to analyze.

A Antecedent	B Behavior	C Consequences

3. Read the following story. Underline the parts of the story you believe to be the Antecedents (A), Behavior (B), and Consequences (C), and label them A, B, C accordingly. Check your responses against those in the Feedback and Answers section. If your analysis was different, look back through the pages of chapter six that describe the A-B-C pattern.

Sam is a twelve-year-old. Sam often demands that his mother give or buy him something or let him go somewhere. Sam asks these things of his mother in a matter-of-fact way, both in his home and outside. When his mother does not give him what he wants immediately, Sam repeats his requests louder and louder. Eventually, he gets very angry and shouts and screams. When he is this angry he also throws things. These episodes occur less often when his father is present. But his demanding is more intense when he is in front of company or in a public place. Mother reacts to such episodes by begging and pleading with Sam not to cause a scene. She also shouts and screams at him to be quiet. Sometimes she gets tired and gives in—more so in public places to avoid embarrassment.

Write your own comments in the space below.

_____

_____

_____

_____

_____

_____

_____

_____

_____

Checking Your Progress

1. Read the following sample situation. Use the A-B-C pattern provided below to analyze this situation. Based on your analysis, what do you think about Johnny's behavior? Write your comments in the spaces below the pattern.

You are the parent of Johnny, a hearing-impaired eight-year-old. Johnny is supposed to go to his room at 4:00 P.M. after school to do his homework. Johnny does not like to do his homework. His teacher says that she has not received his homework for the past week.

You decide to check in on Johnny and find him watching cartoons at 4:00 P.M. in his room and his homework sheets torn up in the wastebasket.

A Antecedents	B Behavior	C Consequences

Write your comments here.

2. True or False

_____ a. A child will repeat a behavior that brings a pleasurable outcome.

_____ b. The antecedent of behavior involves the setting in which the behavior occurs.

_____ c. Words like "fussy" and "stubborn" are good ways to describe behavior because they tell you specifically what the child has done.

_____ d. Consequences happen after the behavior occurs. They include rewards and punishments.

_____ e. The A-B-C pattern is a structured way to analyze the interactions between you and your child.

_____ f. The use of the A-B-C pattern with hearing-impaired children has not proven to be very effective, but it is the only plan available to deal with misbehavior.

_____ g. Ideas and issues taken for granted with hearing children must be made explicit to hearing-impaired children.

_____ h. The A-B-C pattern can be used to develop consistency so a behavior can be changed.

CHAPTER SEVEN

The Rest of the Alphabet

INTRODUCTION

In chapter six you learned a technique for analyzing problem behavior—the A-B-C pattern. You learned that when your child's behavior is examined in the setting in which it occurs, and when you examine what happens after the behavior occurs, then you are better able to determine why the behavior is continuing. The A-B-C pattern helps you discover the best way to change the behavior or stop it from happening. Applying the A-B-C pattern allows you to alter the antecedents and/or consequences, and this can result in a successful behavior change for your child.

This chapter presents details about creating a plan to change your child's problematic behavior using the A-B-C pattern.

Skill Development

> *In order to set up a program for changing a behavior, you must first measure the behavior.*

It is now time to discuss planning a program for behavior change using the A-B-C pattern. The first step is to identify a behavior that may be a problem. Before you can change a behavior, you must first decide whether the behavior is actually a problem for you or your child. After you decide a problem exists, you must describe the behavior in specific terms. It may be helpful to review again the information presented in chapter six so that you can pinpoint the specific behaviors that need change.

In order to set up a program for changing a behavior, you must first measure the behavior to determine how often (frequency) or how long (duration) it occurs (Baker et al., 1976). Measuring the behavior before, during, and after the program begins tells you if the program is working, and can reward you for what you are doing. In other words, keeping track of the behavior can help you judge if you have suppressed your child's problem behavior. If your child's problem behavior is occurring less frequently and less intensely, you have proof a behavior change is occurring. Now let's discuss further the two ways to measure behavior.

1. Frequency: How often the behavior occurs

   Example: Mark has a bad temper. He has several temper tantrums per day. Mark's father counts the number of temper tanrums that occur each day. Some days the father counts four; other days, eight.

2. Duration: How long the behavior occurs

   Example: Sandra rarely comes to dinner when first called.
   Sandra's mother wants to see how long it takes Sandra to come
   to the dinner table each day. After calling Sandra to dinner, her
   mother times Sandra to determine the time between when she
   was first called to when she sits at the table. The times range from
   five to twenty-five minutes for the seven days of the first week.

   How you measure the behavior depends on the characteristics
of the behavior itself. In other words, you decide how to measure
the behavior by counting how often it occurs or by timing how long it
continues when it does occur. Take five minutes to think about the
behaviors listed in the following chart. Mark the chart according to
the best method for measuring the behaviors listed. The first one is
done for you.

Behavior	Frequency (How often?)	Duration (How long?)
1. Clothes left on the floor by a messy child	√ (Count how many times this happens)	
2. Fighting with brothers and sisters		
3. Refusing to obey adults		
4. Daydreaming during a home lesson		
5. Crying episode before bedtime		

   You can record the frequency and duration of the behaviors on a
behavior chart like the one displayed below:

Behavior:			Period of Observation:	_____ Throughout Day _____ Part of Day From _____ to _____ (specify time)				
Sunday	Monday	Tuesday	Wednesday	Thursday	Friday	Saturday	Total	Dates

| Behavior: *hitting brother* | Period of Observation: | ✓ Throughout Day / _____ Part of Day / From _____ to _____ (specify time) | | | | | | |

Sunday	Monday	Tuesday	Wednesday	Thursday	Friday	Saturday	Total	Dates
///	/	////	//	/	///	//	16	6/15-6/21
//	/////	//	/	///	//	////	19	6/22-6/28
/	///	/		//		/	8	6/29-7/5
	//		/			//	5	7/6-7/12

Let's look at an example of how a parent can use a behavior chart. Becky's mother wanted to change Becky's hitting behavior. She measured how often Becky hit her brother during each week. Then, she recorded her observation in the chart above.

Putting information on a graph helps parents see their progress in handling their child's misbehavior. Graphs make your records easy to read and your progress more understandable. Using the example of Becky we will consider how to use a graph in behavior management.

Let us examine the graph to understand how Becky's mother recorded the behavior. The graph has two lines. The vertical line (I) indicates the total number of times (frequency) Becky hit her brother each week. This line begins with zero and stops above the highest number of times the hitting was recorded (in Becky's case, 19, during the second week of observation). The horizontal line (—) indicates the times when the observations were recorded (in Becky's case, each week the behavior was observed).

Program in progress

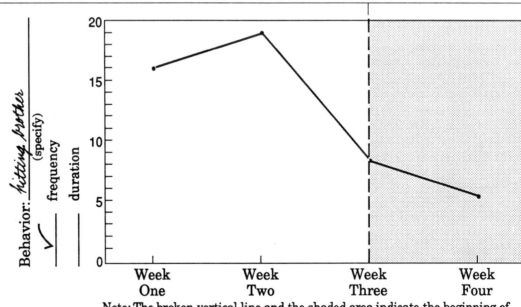

Behavior: *hitting brother* (specify) ⎰ frequency ⎱ duration

Note: The broken vertical line and the shaded area indicate the beginning of the behavior change program.

To make the graph, Becky's mother took the total number of times Becky hit her brother during the first week (16) and placed a dot across this number listed on the vertical line and above the space indicating week one on the horizontal line. Becky's mother continued to make dots on the graph for each total recorded. She then connected the dots to see the pattern of Becky's behavior during the four-week period. As you can see, Becky's mother began a behavior change program during the third week. She can see the results of her program on the graph—Becky's hitting behavior is decreasing.

If you would like to see your results in picture form, you may follow the same procedures as Becky's mother. If you decide not to make a graph, be sure to keep a consistent record of the behavior using a behavior chart.

Any behavior can be measured and charted in the manner just explained. Becky's mother was able to observe and measure her daughter's behavior each day. Your child's behavior, however, may not be similar to Becky's in that it happens too often throughout the day. If the behavior happens so frequently that charting for an entire day is too difficult, you may want to monitor your child's behavior for only certain parts of the day.

You can choose the most convenient manner to measure your child's behavior, either throughout or during a portion of the day. What is important, however, is that you measure the behavior *before beginning the behavior change program*. In the previous example, Becky's mother measured her child's behavior for a period of two weeks before starting a program for behavior change. You may need to measure the behavior for five days, a week, or even two weeks before you begin your behavior change program. This will give you a good idea of *how often* or *how long* the behavior usually occurs. Later, having obtained this measure, you can judge if the program is working—if the behavior is decreasing. Now let us examine the remaining parts of the A-B-C pattern that you will use in developing a program for behavior change.

Any behavior can be measured and charted.

The Remaining Parts of the A-B-C Pattern

Specifying and measuring the problem behavior are only the first steps in beginning your program. Next look at the consequences placed on your child's behavior. Consequences (what happens after the behavior occurs) can sometimes be arranged and changed more easily than can the antecedents (the setting in which the behavior occurs).

Consequences, for the most part, involve the use of rewards (pleasant outcomes) and punishments (unpleasant outcomes). Once you've identified the consequence for a specific behavior, focus on how to remove the pleasant outcomes that reinforce that inappropriate behavior. The three most frequently used consequences to decrease problem behavior are 1) ignoring the behavior; 2) punishing the behavior; and 3) giving time out.

Ignoring a behavior removes the attention that serves to reward your child for misbehaving. For example, if your child cries when put to bed, the crying will gradually decrease and eventually stop if the behavior (the crying) is ignored. If a brother continuously teases his sister and she learns to ignore her brother's comments, the

Ignoring a Behavior

teasing will gradually decrease and eventually stop. Thus, ignoring the behavior tells the child that no reward or reinforcement will follow the misbehavior.

Certain behaviors, however, cannot be ignored because they are harmful to the child or others. For example, it would be unwise to ignore a child who hits himself or herself or others. Alternatives to ignoring would be in order.

Punishing a Behavior

Punishment removes a reward (reinforcement) or places a negative consequence on behavior. Removing a reward from a child is an effective way to reduce the occurrence of problem behaviors. This technique is most effective when, after removing a reward, you give your child a way to earn back the reinforcer (Baker et al., 1976; Canter & Canter, 1985). This way your child does not fear or avoid you when you are punishing. Also, your child is encouraged to practice the appropriate behavior in order to regain the reward. You should also warn your child to stop the misbehavior before you punish.

Example:
Parent: "Sue, I cannot allow you to poke and hit your brother when you play together. If you poke your brother, you will choose to sit in the corner. It's your choice."

Sue: "Okay." (Continues to poke and hit).

Parent: "Sue, you poked your brother. You have made a choice to sit in the corner and not play. Tomorrow you can try again to play correctly with your brother."

Punishment, such as the removal of a reinforcer, should be used as a second choice to reinforcement. Always try to reinforce appropriate behavior before using punishment. Appropriate behaviors that are incompatible with the misbehavior should be rewarded. In other words, reinforce appropriate behavior that is opposite of the misbehavior. The child cannot act appropriately and misbehave at the same time. Appropriate behavior is incompatible with misbehavior. Let us look at the example of Sue once again. The following day...

Always try to reinforce appropriate behavior before using punishment.

Parent: "Sue, I like the way you and your brother are playing. You are sharing and playing nicely together."

Sue: "I like to play with Jon."

Parent: "Because you are playing so well you can play an extra five minutes today."

Sue's parent saw her using appropriate play behavior. Sue was reinforced for displaying appropriate behavior that is incompatible with the poking and hitting behaviors seen earlier. If Sue is rewarded for good playing behavior, this behavior will likely continue. And if Sue is playing well, she cannot misbehave. Therefore, by reinforcing her good playing behavior, she is unlikely to continue her previous misbehavior.

The time-out procedure is another way to reduce inappropriate behavior. Time out removes the child from the rewards that are given by being around other persons or rewarding objects. The child is removed from the reinforcing situation (by being placed in the corner or in another room) after he or she misbehaves. To be effective, time out must be given immediately and without fuss. The length of time for time out should be determined before the child is removed. This time should not exceed five minutes (Baker et al., 1976).

Again, this technique means time out from the opportunity to be rewarded (receive a reinforcer). A separate room, corner, or chair are all effective time-out places. This technique should only be used if the other two methods—ignoring and punishing the misbehavior—do not stop the unwanted behavior.

The principles related to the use of time out are as follows:

1. Explain to the child about the time out in advance. Specify what behaviors are cause for time out; where time out is located; how long the time out will last. Give your child expectations about what will happen.

2. Do not argue with your child about assigning time out. Use as few words as possible. Say "time out" or point in the direction of the time-out area.

3. Do not respond to your child while in the time-out area. Respond only after the designated time has been completed and your child has behaved appropriately.

4. Do not call attention to the incident when time out is over.

5. After the child has completed time out, praise or reward the child for appropriate behavior.

Giving Time Out

Example:
Carl has a habit of biting his brother whenever they watch television together. Carl's mother and father explain that he is not to bite his brother. Carl continues. The parents now tell him that biting is not appropriate under any circumstances. They also clearly state that Carl will be given a three-minute time-out period if he continues biting. Time out is designated to be a corner in the room clear of all toys or interesting material.

Carl continues to bite his brother as they watch their favorite cartoon. Carl's mother immediately says, "Carl, you bit your brother. You have chosen time out." He begins to cry, and says, "It won't happen again." Mother responds by pointing to the time-out area. Carl goes to time out. After three minutes, Carl's mother allows him to again watch television. She later praises him for how well he is watching television with his brother.

Only you can decide on the best consequences for a given problem behavior. Remember, remove the reward that keeps your child misbehaving. Many times the payoff (reward) is *attention*. The child receives attention when misbehavior occurs. Ignoring, removing a reward, or time out are effective consequences for preventing and stopping misbehavior.

You can oftentimes prevent or stop a misbehavior by changing the setting (the antecedents).

Example:
A father knows his child and a neighbor child both like the same toy (the antecedent). He removes the toy from the play area before the children enter.

Example:
A mother is aware that her child usually is very tired after school. During this time, the child is easily frustrated, irritated, and extremely argumentative. The mother directs the child to take a nap (the antecedent) before continuing the day.

The importance of antecedent events is illustrated in the following example:
The mother of a five-year-old child is distraught because of her son's temper tantrums. She applies the A-B-C pattern to carefully analyze her son's behavior. The mother observes that each time she asks her son to do something when he is involved in an activity, he does not respond. As the mother continues to talk, her voice grows louder and louder as her son ignores her requests. When the mother finally reaches her limit, she puts away the play material. The little boy then has a tantrum.

After deciding to use the A-B-C pattern, the mother begins to analyze the situation. It becomes obvious to the mother that the play items distract the boy from responding. The mother decides to

Remove the reward that keeps your child misbehaving.

You and Your Hearing-Impaired Child

rearrange the antecedents to prevent the tantrum behavior from occurring. She makes sure all distracting items such as toys, television, and books are out of sight or not near the child when she (the mother) wants to teach her son how to respond appropriately. She then reinforces her son whenever he responds in the appropriate manner.

We have discussed the application of the A-B-C pattern to reduce or stop unwanted behaviors. It is very important that we also promote appropriate behaviors. For example, we not only want to stop Mary Jane from hitting her dog, but we also want to reinforce (reward) her for playing nicely and gently with her dog. Appendix 1 lists possible reinforcers available to parents. Add to the list as you experience the specific consequences that are reinforcing to your child.

> *Parents must become detectives as they interact with their children.*

Applications

Parents must become detectives as they interact with their children. Problem behaviors are nothing more than the successful ways your child has learned to get what he or she wants from the environment (Baker et al., 1976). In hearing-impaired children, however, these behaviors may also represent ways to communicate wants and needs to others. In order to do your detective work thoroughly and completely, you must examine the A-B-C pattern from your hearing-impaired child's point of view. To you, behaviors such as screaming and chasing are not pleasant consequences. To your hearing-impaired child these consequences may be reinforcing because they cause you to respond—to give your child attention. As we know, behaviors that are followed by positive reinforcers are more likely to happen again.

Applying the A-B-C pattern to the behavior of hearing-impaired children is done in the same manner as with hearing children. However, there are a few considerations that you might want to keep in mind.

Antecedents

In many instances, when antecedents are changed, the misbehaviors decrease. To illustrate this point, let's take the example of a father of a hearing-impaired seven-year-old boy.

Example:
The family moves into a new home. Since the move, the hearing-impaired boy cries and appears frightened when it is time for bed. This behavior occurs at least four times per week. The boy's father decides he and his son will look at a storybook at bedtime in order to tire the boy. To the father's surprise, the crying episodes increase rather than decrease.

An examination of the settings in which the behavior occurs reveals that the crying never happened at the old house. In the previous home, the boy's room was positioned in the opposite direction from his new room. It faced the street and was dimly lit by streetlights. The new room faces the backyard and has no source of light. This room is very dark when the lights are off.

In the dark silence, the boy is not aware that his parents are nearby. Hence, he cries when he does not immediately fall

asleep. The boy's father thinks his presence is needed to give the boy security. However, the attention received from the father increases rather than decreases the behavior. Placing a night light outside the boy's room enables him to fall asleep and decreases the crying episodes.

You must carefully examine the impact of hearing impairment on the antecedents of behavior. Try to discover how hearing impairment influences the situation or the antecedent events. Only then can you properly alter the events in your hearing-impaired child's life. In the previous example, the child's hearing loss blocked out all auditory information. Therefore, when the lights were out, the boy experienced a sense of being totally alone. The light from the night light provided the boy with assurance that his parents were nearby.

Behavior

Some behaviors are common to hearing-impaired children. You must become aware of these types of behaviors.

Example:
A four-year-old hearing-impaired child makes several shrill noises when she is unable to watch television. The mother usually gives her more time to watch television in order to stop her daughter's shrieking. The shrieking continues and even increases during times other than when the child wants to watch television. She displays the shrieking behavior while playing, when eating, etc. The mother decides she needs a program to decrease this annoying behavior. She begins by counting the frequency of the shrieking behavior for one week.

Behavior: *shrieking*			Period of Observation:		_____ Throughout Day			
					√ Part of Day			
					From 3:00 P.M. to 6:00 P.M. (specify time)			
Sunday	Monday	Tuesday	Wednesday	Thursday	Friday	Saturday	Total	Dates
√√√√	√√√	√√√√	√√√√√ √√√√	√√√√√	√√√√ √√	√√√√ √√	44 (Average of 6 per day)	

The mother then decides that she needs to use a program involving time out (removal of the child from the situation so no reinforcement can occur). She uses this technique consistently. She also attempts to reinforce appropriate behavior when the shrieking behavior does not occur. The mother demonstrates to the daughter the proper ways to watch television, have a snack, or play during the times that are appropriate for such activities. The mother also makes a picture board for each day's scheduled events. When the child appropriately points to the picture when it is time for the activity, she is rewarded. The girl is also rewarded (by points) for appropriate behavior during the specific activity. With these extra points, she is able to buy more time to do the activity during that day or later.

The shrieking behavior displayed by the girl in the above example results from the child's inability to communicate her wants and needs effectively. Her mother determines that this behavior is annoying and in need of elimination. Some problem behaviors exhibited by hearing-impaired children may result from their inability to communicate. It may be necessary to target these behaviors for change and to replace them by teaching the child more appropriate methods for communicating wants and needs.

Consequences

Consequences can be changed to decrease misbehavior. An example of a grandmother interacting with her six-year-old grandchild will illustrate this point.

Example:
A six-year-old hearing-impaired boy hits his grandmother whenever he wants her attention. The hit is not forceful or harmful but it is annoying. The grandmother explains to the boy, through demonstration, that hitting is not appropriate. She tells him she will not listen to him or look at him if she is hit. He will receive attention only if he gains her eye contact and uses proper ways to signal her. She also uses the consequence of ignoring if he hits her to ask for something or to express a need. She only responds to an emergency. The grandmother also decides to teach her grandson the appropriate skills needed to gain the attention of others.

Whenever the child practices these skills or uses appropriate methods, he is given positive consequences and is rewarded

Some problem behaviors exhibited by hearing-impaired children may result from their inability to communicate.

for his behavior with praise at the moment and given stickers at the end of the day. In time, the child not only decreases his hitting behavior, but increases his use of the new skills learned for getting others' attention.

Remember to replace the inappropriate behaviors with alternative behaviors. This will enable the child to practice appropriate ways of behaving. At times it may seem difficult to apply the needed consequences consistently because of the nature of the hearing-impaired condition. But in order for your plan to work, consequences must be enforced consistently. *Long-term gains far outweigh short-term displeasures.*

The examples given illustrate three important points to remember when using the A-B-C pattern with hearing-impaired children:

In order for your plan to work, consequences must be enforced consistently.

1. Examine the antecedents in relation to your child's hearing impairment. Is the setting appropriate for your child to receive or give messages? Is there something in your child's environment that increases the occurrence of a problem behavior because of his or her hearing impairment?

2. Examine your child's behavior in relation to his or her hearing impairment. Does your child lack the communication skills needed to convey wants and needs? Could this bring on the misbehavior? Teaching your child ways to express wants or needs with signing, gestures, pictures, etc., may ease the frustration. Also, annoying behaviors may result directly from the impact of the hearing-impaired condition (e.g., making loud noises). Simple demonstration or explanation sometimes alleviates these problem behaviors.

3. Do not assume that your child can make the connection between your rules and the behaviors you deem appropriate or the consequences you give. Connections between behaviors and consequences must be made *explicitly*. Demonstrate for your child before and following episodes of misbehavior all that is important to the situation. Be sure your child understands the connections. Visual and tactile methods may provide the proof a hearing-impaired child needs to make a logical connection between behaviors and consequences. The use of logical consequences (see chapter five) can also help your child to understand these connections.

Parent and Child

This section contains examples of parents who have used the A-B-C pattern successfully with their hearing-impaired children. First, the parents analyzed the behavior using the A-B-C pattern. Second, they decided to change the antecedents and consequences to decrease and/ or stop the misbehavior. Although not shown here, the parents measured, charted, and graphed the child's behavior in need of change.

Lois is a seven-year-old hearing-impaired child who does not comply with her parents' wishes. For example, she refuses to do some household chores when asked. The parents decide to use the A-B-C pattern to analyze her misbehavior. The results of their analysis are as follows:

A Antecedent	B Behavior	C Consequences
Mother requests that Lois clean up her room on a Saturday afternoon. Lois is playing outside. She is brought into her room.	Lois shakes her head and closes her eyes. She tries to leave the room, refusing to do her chore.	Lois is kept in her room until she does the chore.

After analyzing this behavior pattern, Lois's parents discover that they can change the antecedents and consequences of her behavior. They believe that changing these parts of the pattern will reduce Lois's noncompliant behavior. The parents decide to arrange a designated time each week for Lois to do her chores. This time will be arranged on a consistent basis (the same time each week). Also, Lois will do her chores *before* she plays. The antecedent (mother making a request while the child was playing) helped prevent Lois from behaving appropriately. Also, the parents believe it is important to keep Lois from playing (consequence) until her chore is completed. Lois will remain in the house until she follows the request. They believe a positive consequence should be given when Lois behaves appropriately. They decide to reinforce Lois with extra playtime when she completes her expected work.

David is a hearing-impaired youngster, three years of age. David has developed a habit of biting other children. His biting behavior occurs when he is playing or working beside children in his preschool group. David's father is frustrated with his son's behavior. The father became concerned when a parent told her child to bite David back to show him how it feels. David's father realizes something must be done. He decides to use the A-B-C pattern. This pattern is a summary of several patterns observed over time.

A Antecedent	B Behavior	C Consequences
Biting occurs when another child is using something David wants (crayon, toy, swing at the playground, etc.). David first attempts to get another child's attention by hitting.	David bites children at play and in preschool.	Children ignore David's attempts at getting what he wants. Children cry, scream, and sometimes hit David. An adult comes to the other child's rescue. David gets what he wants while attention is on the other child.

David's father reviews the information gathered from the A-B-C pattern. He decides that the consequences to David's behavior must be altered immediately. David's father and his teacher designate a time-out area for David during the preschool period. David is shown explicitly that biting is not appropriate through demonstration.

David's father also draws a picture of a younger child biting another child and indicates his disapproval. This picture is placed in the time-out area. Every time David is seen biting another child, David is placed immediately in time out for three minutes. The adult shows David the picture of the limit and firmly shakes his or her head, No!

David's father believes that his son is not aware of appropriate behaviors for expressing his wants. David responds quickly without thinking about his behavior. Reviewing the antecedents, his father sees that David does try to get the child's attention first before biting. He decides to teach his child appropriate ways of communicating his wants and needs to others. David's father knows that in addition to using the consequence of time out for his son's misbehavior, he must also reinforce David for appropriate behaviors towards other children.

Points to Remember

To stop or prevent a misbehavior from occurring, you must remove the reward that keeps the child misbehaving.

1. When observing the behavior of a child for behavior change, you must do three things: determine if behavior is a problem; describe the behavior in specific terms; and measure the behavior.

2. You can measure the behavior in two ways: by determining its frequency (how often a behavior occurs) or its duration (how long the behavior occurs).

3. Measure the behavior before, during, and after the program begins to determine whether your program is working.

4. Consequences, for the most part, involve rewards (pleasant outcomes) and punishments (unpleasant outcomes). The three most frequently used consequences to decrease problem behavior are ignoring a behavior; punishing a behavior; and giving time out.

5. To stop or prevent a misbehavior from occurring, you must remove the reward that keeps the child misbehaving. Many times the payoff (reward) is attention. The child receives attention when misbehavior occurs.

6. You can prevent or stop a misbehavior by changing the setting.

7. Problem behaviors are successful ways your child has learned to get what he or she wants from the environment.

8. Applying the A-B-C pattern to the behavior of hearing-impaired children is done in the same manner as with hearing children. You must, however, examine the A-B-C pattern from your hearing-impaired child's point of view.

9. Replace the inappropriate behaviors with alternative behaviors. This will enable your child to practice appropriate behavior.

10. The nature of the hearing-impaired condition may make it difficult to apply the needed consequences consistently. In order for your plan to work, consequences must be enforced consistently. Long-term gains far outweigh short-term displeasures.

1. Before you change a child's behavior, you must observe it. The first step is to decide what behavior you will examine. Next, count the behaviors. You can do this by measuring how often or how long the behavior occurs. Choose three behaviors that you see in your child. These may be appropriate or inappropriate behaviors. Write these behaviors in the chart below. Now decide how you will measure this behavior and mark the chart accordingly.

Behavior	Frequency (How often?)	Duration (How long?)
1.		
2.		
3.		

2. To get experience observing and measuring behavior, choose a behavior that you often see in your child. Take ten minutes each day during the next two weeks and observe your child during an activity when this behavior is likely to occur. Write your observations on the behavior chart. After the two weeks, record your results on the graph provided.

Behavior: _____

Period of Observation: _____ Throughout Day _____ Part of Day   From _____ to _____ (specify time)

Sunday	Monday	Tuesday	Wednesday	Thursday	Friday	Saturday	Total	Dates

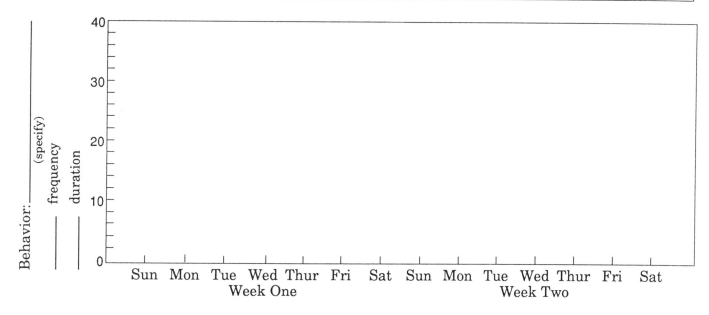

3. Select a problem behavior of your child, observe, and measure it. Follow the steps below.

   a. Specify the problem behavior.

   _____

   b. How will you measure the behavior? (Check one)

   _____ Frequency (How often)

   _____ Duration (How long)

   c. When will you observe the behavior?

   _____ Throughout day (happens infrequently)

   _____ Part of day (happens frequently)
   _____ to _____ (Specify time)

Observe and measure child's problem behavior throughout the next two weeks. Record your observations in the chart below.

Behavior:			Period of Observation: _____ Throughout Day _____ Part of Day From _____ to _____ (specify time)					
Sunday	Monday	Tuesday	Wednesday	Thursday	Friday	Saturday	Total	Dates

You are now ready to arrange the consequences and/or antecedents to change behavior. You may want to experiment with this in weeks to come. Continue to measure the behavior and graph your results so you can see your progress. You can save the information obtained in this activity for use in working with chapter nine.

1. Read the sample problem below. What would you do in this situation? Complete the information needed below to begin a program of behavior change.

David teases his sister throughout the day. Sometimes he teases her so much by calling her names, telling her he is going to hit her, etc., that she comes to you crying. You decide you must prevent or stop this behavior from occurring.

a. Specify the problem behavior.

_____

b. How will you measure the behavior?

_____ Frequency (How many)

_____ Duration (How long)

c. When will you observe the behavior?

_____ Throughout day (happens infrequently)

_____ Part of day (happens frequently)

_____ to _____ (Specify time of day)

d. Describe how you will measure David's behavior. Use the following example as a guide.

When changing Marie's behavior, I will watch her while she gets ready for dinner. Fifteen minutes before dinnertime, I will record how long it takes Marie to sit at the table from the time I first called her.

_____

_____

_____

_____

_____

_____

_____

_____

_____

_____

_____

2. True or False

_____ a. The first step in changing behavior is to place consequences on the child.

_____ b. Duration is a measure of how long a behavior occurs.

_____ c. Ignoring a behavior removes the attention that serves to reward your child for misbehavior.

_____ d. Punishing a behavior removes the child from a situation that is reinforcing. A separate room, corner, or a chair are all effective punishment places.

_____ e. The child should understand the causes for time out, where it is located, and how long it will last, before time out is administered.

_____ f. Using the A-B-C pattern to change behavior involves detective-like work.

_____ g. It is not important to replace unwanted behavior with appropriate behaviors because the child will naturally practice appropriate behavior after the inappropriate behavior has stopped.

_____ h. You must explain limits, consequences, and the connections between them explicitly to your hearing-impaired child.

CHAPTER EIGHT

Nonverbal Behavior

INTRODUCTION

Chapters five, six, and seven introduced information about behavior management. They presented specific principles for controlling your child's misbehavior. Two such principles are setting firm and consistent limits and providing consequences that relate directly to the misbehavior. Information was also presented on how to use the A-B-C pattern to prevent or stop severe problem behaviors. The information presented will help you discipline effectively. When you discipline, you are communicating with your child. Hence, discipline is a communication process.

When you think of communication, you probably think of speaking, listening, reading, or writing. Our language is, however, both verbal (involving words) and nonverbal. We may smile, frown, look angry, or look pleased depending on the situation. Our body communicates nonverbally how we feel and adds to what we are saying. For example, a young baby is happy and smiling in her mother's arms. As soon as the mother lays the baby down, the infant cries. The child is telling the mother, nonverbally, she would rather be held. Another example is a man who stands in a lunch line. The server asks if he wants liver and onions. The man gives the server a nasty facial expression and points to the roast beef. The server knows exactly what the man would like to eat even though he has not spoken a single word.

Gestures, facial expressions, and other forms of body language all add meaning to what you communicate. Parents and children use nonverbal communication every day to express their wishes and desires. The use of nonverbal communication is critical in the lives of all individuals—hearing and nonhearing alike. The parents of hearing-impaired children, perhaps even unknowingly, use non-verbal communication continually, but they may not be aware that nonverbal communication plays a crucial part in the behavior management of children.

This chapter will help you become aware of the importance of nonverbal communication. As you read and complete the exercises provided, you will become better prepared to use nonverbal skills in a purposeful way with your hearing-impaired child.

Skill Development

The communication process is both verbal and nonverbal (Walters, 1982). Our actions, facial expressions, and body movements all

> *Gestures, facial expressions, and other forms of body language all add meaning to what you communicate.*

communicate to others whether we are listening, enjoying what is happening, or engaging in an activity.

Communication is a way of sharing ideas and feelings. A large portion of all human communication is nonverbal. Most people transmit and read body language. For the most part, however, they do it unknowingly (Ogden & Lipsett, 1982). For example, let's say that a man you know is giving a speech to a large audience. Before beginning, he fidgets with materials on the table in front of him, looks through his notes, straightens his tie, and shifts his eyes back and forth. Because you know this individual is competent, you probably dismiss all of these nonverbal cues. Another person attending the same meeting does not know of the speaker's competence. That observer probably will be more aware of the speaker's uncomfortable and nervous behaviors.

Nonverbal communication supplements verbal communication. In other words, what we do through our actions and expressions adds to what we say—gives extra meaning to it. The use of gestures, facial expressions, and other forms of body language give extra meaning to the spoken word. Nonverbal language is an extremely potent part of communication. In fact, it has been estimated that only 35 percent of the meaning of a social conversation is given by the words actually spoken (Birdwhistell, as cited in Davis, 1973).

There are obviously thousands of types of nonverbal behaviors that can be listed and discussed (Walters, 1982). These behaviors can be placed into three main groups: gestures, facial expressions, and body language. Other individuals may group these nonverbal behaviors differently. And some may put them all in the one category called "body language." Whatever the category or grouping system used, it is apparent that nonverbal behaviors are an extremely important part of our communication system.

Gestures

Gestures involve moving the hands, head, or other parts of the body while speaking (*Correspondence Course*, 1983). Gestures help others understand what you are saying and can emphasize the spoken word. This form of nonverbal communication can also be used in place of a whole sentence or a paragraph of words.

Some examples of gestures are telling a little child it's time for bed simply by putting your head on your hands and pointing to the bedroom, waving hello, holding your hand up to someone talking (which indicates that you've heard enough), and waving your finger to indicate the behavior was not the correct way to act.

Facial Expressions

Facial expressions add meaning to your words. Your face gives important cues to your true feelings. Often you may be preoccupied or unaware that your facial expression does not match your words or actions. For example, you are in a store and your child throws a tantrum. You look around and smile as you tell the child that this is not appropriate behavior (*Correspondence Course*, 1983; Ogden & Lipsett, 1982).

Some examples of facial expressions are smiling, frowning, wrinkling the forehead (may indicate worry), pouting, and biting your lip.

Body language is a set of nonverbal cues given by the body. These cues support our feelings and words. Body language may differ from culture to culture, but several types of communication have definite meanings that most people understand or pick up naturally.

Some examples of body language are making eye contact (means interest, attention), looking at another person but looking away when they return your glance (shyness, or keeping distance), blushing (embarrassment), leaning forward when someone is talking (display interest), and hanging the head or looking at the ground (sadness, guilt).

Nonverbal Communication and Discipline

Both adults and children use nonverbal communication to express themselves. Children have a natural talent for nonverbal language (Ogden, 1984). In their little world, children roam about seeking boundaries through their senses. They look, listen, touch, taste, and smell to learn about their environment.

Children tune into our facial expressions and gestures at an early age. It is important to understand the power of nonverbal communication as you interact within your family. Nonverbal communication is a powerful tool when you try to teach your children the proper ways of behaving. Discipline is a communication process and nonverbal communication is a vital part of that process.

Proper use of nonverbal techniques helps add consistency to your discipline. If you use appropriate nonverbal behaviors with your spoken words, you will send clear, consistent messages that cannot be misinterpreted. You may sometimes be unaware that your body movements or facial expressions are inconsistent with the message you are trying to convey. For example, your child comes up to you during an important dinner party gathering and asks to go outside. You politely say "No" and point to the play area and nod your approval. Your child goes to the play area and begins to make a tremendous amount of noise. You go to your child and communicate that the noise is not appropriate. Because this is happening in front of your friends, you look nervously at your child and say "Stop." Your child picks up that your facial expression and your body language are not giving firm support to your words. Your child continues to make noise.

A large portion of all human communication is nonverbal.

Remember that your child does not understand that you are embarrassed or that you are trying to save face. Your child is simply reading your nonverbal cues in addition to your spoken words. Children attend to the information that they find *usually* explains the meaning of the words, that is, the nonverbal behaviors of their parents.

You must practice using nonverbal behaviors in order to send clear and consistent messages to your child. And finally, using nonverbal praise is extremely important in your interactions with your child. A hug, smile, wink, or a pat on the back can all communicate more than several "goods" or "nice jobs." These nonverbal behaviors all let your child know that you support and recognize his or her appropriate behaviors.

Listed below are guidelines for using nonverbal behaviors effectively.

Guidelines for Use of Nonverbal Behaviors

> *Nonverbal praise is extremely important in your interactions with your child.*

1. Stay calm. Be careful not to scream, yell, or force your requests. By staying calm, you communicate to your child that you are in control.

2. Look your child in the eyes when you speak. Eye contact is important to human communication. We say as much with our eyes as with our words. You can increase the effectiveness of your messages with eye contact.

3. Emphasize your words with gestures. Hand gestures often communicate nonverbally to the child, "I mean what I'm saying." Remember, however, that there is a difference between a hand gesture designed to emphasize your words and one used to intimidate your child (e.g., shaking your finger in your child's face).

4. Touch your child. Touch creates a physical as well as verbal limit. As you speak, gently place your hand on your child as a clear indication of your caring and your sincerity.
(Adapted from Canter & Canter, 1985, pp. 17-18.)

Applications

Dr. Paul Ogden, a profoundly deaf professional, has related the following experience from his childhood. The story represents the usefulness and the complexity of nonverbal communication:

> When he was twelve years old, his brother took him to an airport to meet his parents on an incoming flight. While waiting for the plane, his brother sat across from a row of doorless telephone booths. All, for the moment, were occupied. As Paul scanned the line of men talking on the phones, he could tell which men were enjoying their conversations and which were not, which were talking with people they liked or loved and which were talking with strangers or business associates, which were nervous about what they were saying and which were talking naturally. He could even speculate about which men were lying and which were telling the truth. (Ogden & Lipsett, 1982, p. 75)

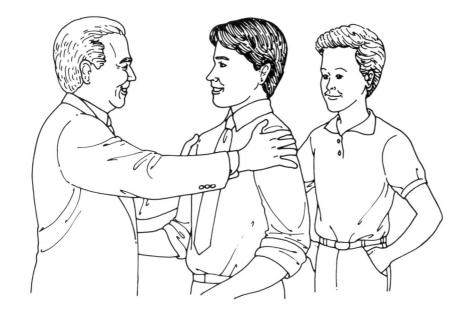

How much more could a person have learned without listening to the actual conversations of these men?

Nonverbal communication is a way of sharing information and feelings. But as Ogden's story illustrates, nonverbal communication can tell you much more than verbal communication alone. In many ways, nonverbal communication adds meaning and verifies what you say and do.

Hearing impairment affects hearing and speech, but not the ability to communicate. Hearing-impaired children have their hands, arms, faces, and eyes, and they will seek ways to communicate (Ogden & Lipsett, 1982).

Communication is a natural impulse for any human being. Children have a natural ability for nonverbal communication. Hearing-impaired children are no exception. Nonverbal communication should be viewed as a hearing-impaired child's innate talent to express him- or herself. This does not mean that nonverbal communication should be used instead of verbal language. Nonverbal communication supplements and enhances these forms of communication.

A hearing-impaired child tunes in early to your facial expressions, your body movements, and the cues given by your eyes. It is just as important for you to cue into your child's nonverbal language as it is for you to practice your own nonverbal language skills. Cuing into your hearing-impaired child's nonverbal language will give you a better understanding of your child's behavior. The following example will illustrate this point.

A hearing-impaired three-year-old boy is playing with his favorite truck and puts it away in the closet. Two days later he wants to play with his truck but cannot remember where he put it. His mother is ironing in the other room. The little boy runs up to his mother frantically gesturing for her to come and help him look for the truck. The mother asks the boy clearly, "What do you want?" The boy, in tears, continues to gesture to the playroom but is unable to communicate effectively that he has lost his truck. The mother, thinking that the boy wants to play, tells him to go ahead and play; she points to the room and nods her head. The boy, now frustrated, bursts into tears, and throws a temper tantrum, for which the mother punishes him and sends him to his room.

This story gives an example of what can happen when a parent does not tune into the nonverbal cues of her child. The mother picks up only on the boy's insistent pointing behavior to the playroom, and does not pick up on his worrisome looks and his shrugging shoulders. The boy's nonverbal behavior is a sign of his losing something rather than a request to do something. Remember to cue into the nonverbal language of your hearing-impaired child to understand the message being communicated.

Just as your child's nonverbal cues are important, your nonverbal communication is extremely important to your child. Your facial expressions, body movements and eye contact are all pieces of meaningful information to your hearing-impaired child. Do not hold back these important sources of information. Holding back can only hinder your child in accurately receiving your verbal messages. Hearing-impaired children need all the cues they can get to clearly receive your messages. For example, eye movements communicate excitement, pain, happiness, sadness, doubt, etc. Maintaining eye contact with your hearing-impaired child provides the visual cues necessary for him or her to understand the tone in your voice (which is available to hearing people). The eyes can communicate your mood to an individual aware of nonverbal cues (Ogden & Lipsett, 1982). Inhibiting yourself from using gestures, body movements, and eye contact will prevent your child from getting to know you and from understanding your messages. Parents who have both hearing and hearing-impaired children often are more expressive with their hearing children (*Correspondence Course*, 1983; Ogden & Lipsett, 1982). Remember to be naturally expressive with all of your children. If the content of this chapter helps you become more aware of the importance of nonverbal communication in the lives of all children, especially the hearing-impaired, it has accomplished its task.

This book has included a discussion of the use of several techniques to control your hearing-impaired child's behavior. Nonverbal communication is a technique that gives clarity to what you say or do, and also helps you develop consistency as a behavior manager. Your ultimate goal is to send a clear, consistent message that cannot be misinterpreted by your child. Awareness of nonverbal cues can help you in this goal.

Consistency is an important area of concern for the parents of hearing-impaired children, since confusion is inevitable when the body and the intended message contradict each other. When you are not in total control of your body (when you feel tired or apathetic), your body movements can be inconsistent with the message you are trying to convey. Remember that your child is well-versed in the meanings of your expressions, gestures, and postures. When you are tense and feeling uneasy, your child looks beyond your smile and notices the feelings in your eyes and facial expressions. Since the hearing-impaired child is in tune with your nonverbal methods of communication, you must back up your words with meaningful nonverbal cues.

> *Confusion is inevitable when the body and the intended message contradict each other.*

Techniques to Enhance the Effectiveness of Nonverbal Communication

There are specific techniques that can help you clearly communicate your nonverbal messages to your hearing-impaired child.

1. Communicate with your child at eye level. Kneeling down will enable you to make direct contact with your hearing-impaired child.

2. Eye cues give subtle meanings to your verbal messages. Stay aware of your head movements in order to make it easy for your eyes to be seen by your child.

3. Be as responsive as possible with your face and body to all of your hearing-impaired child's messages. The hearing-impaired child needs nonverbal cues from you to indicate you are listening and understanding.

4. Use gestures as much as possible, and make your gestures as normal as possible. Many gestures are universal and can be understood by your child.

5. Refine your body language as your child gets older. The older the child, the more subtle and complex the cues become. (Adapted from Ogden & Lipsett, 1982, pp. 69-70).

> *Remember to cue into the nonverbal language of your hearing-impaired child to understand the message being communicated.*

Parent and Child

Listed below are several examples of nonverbal communications that convey certain meanings to your hearing-impaired child. These communications are examples of ways to let your child know what you mean through the use of your eyes, facial expressions, and body movements. These examples demonstrate that nonverbal communication is a very powerful tool for behavior management as well as everyday conversation.

Verbal Communication	Nonverbal Communication
"No! That is not acceptable."	Look very displeased and shake head from side to side. Be very firm and rigid in your facial expressions and posture. Touch child, act out the misbehavior if necessary, and again firmly shake your head from side to side.
"What are you doing?"	Point to the child with a questioning look on face. Shrug your shoulders and point to activity in question.
"What is wrong?	Show a worried look on your face with a questioning expression. Point to child. Touch the child to show you care while using a questioning expression.

"Good job, well done!"	Smile and look pleased. Touch the child and point to what he or she has done to please you. Act out behavior if necessary. Let your whole body, arms, shoulders, face, etc., show your happiness.
"Which do you want?"	Show or act out options. Use questioning expression. Point to both choices and then to the child.

(Adapted from Ogden & Lipsett, 1982, pp. 70-75; and Walters, 1982).

Points to Remember

1. When you think of communication, you probably think of speaking, listening, reading, and writing. Our language is, however, both verbal (involving words) and nonverbal.

2. Gestures, facial expressions, and other forms of body language all add meaning to what you communicate. The use of nonverbal communication is critical in the lives of all individuals—hearing and nonhearing alike.

3. Nonverbal communication supplements verbal communication. In other words, what we do through our actions and expressions adds to what we say—gives extra meaning to it.

4. Children have a natural ability for nonverbal language. Children often learn and express themselves through nonverbal communication.

5. Nonverbal behaviors can help parents send clear and consistent messages to children.

6. Nonverbal praise is extremely important in interactions with children. A hug, smile, a wink—all let your child know that you support and recognize his or her appropriate behaviors.

7. Nonverbal communication should be viewed as a hearing-impaired child's innate talent for self-expression.

8. Nonverbal communication should not be used instead of speech or verbal language; it supplements these forms of communication.

9. Your facial expressions, body movements, and eye contact are important sources of information to your hearing-impaired child. Do not hold back these important sources of information from your child.

1. Think about greeting a friend that you haven't seen for ten years without using nonverbal body language. Write down your comments about the picture you have in your mind.

   Consider this: If you only use your voice, the old friend may receive your message as a snub or an unenthusiastic greeting.

_____

_____

_____

_____

_____

2. Spend time in front of the mirror to determine what messages you are sending to others. Use the chart below to see what gestures and expressions you would use to match the message you wish to convey. Look at yourself in front of the mirror as you act out these nonverbal behaviors. This may seem a little embarrassing to you at first, but it will give you an idea of how important nonverbal messages can be. This activity is not used to teach you how to create nonverbal messages, but to help you to become aware of how you already use them. Write your comments in the chart.

Nonverbal Behaviors

1. You are very pleased.	Comments:
2. You are trying to figure out a complex problem.	Comments:
3. You are worried about an outcome of a situation.	Comments:
4. You are firm and consistent about a rule you have set for your child.	Comments:

3. During one day of this week, choose thirty minutes to watch people around you. This can be done during a lunch break from the office or on your way to church, in a restaurant, etc. Observe the nonverbal communication taking place during several different interactions. Note if the individuals seem happy, sad, bored, etc. Make mental notes about all of the forms of nonverbal communication you observe. After you observe for half an hour, take five minutes to write down your observations.

_____

_____

_____

_____

_____

_____

_____

_____

_____

4. Review the techniques about communicating your nonverbal messages. Choose a variety of situations to actively use these techniques with your child. Write down comments you have after you use these techniques.

_____

_____

_____

_____

_____

_____

_____

_____

_____

_____

1. Read the sample problem below. What do you think was the reason for Mary's behavior?

   Mary is twelve years old and has a mild hearing loss. She occasionally likes to turn up the volume of the stereo in the dining room to hear some of her music tapes. Mary's father is entertaining business guests in the den located two rooms away from the dining area. Mary turns up the stereo when she arrives home from school. Mary's father and his business associates are startled and come into the dining room. Mary's father, embarrassed and smiling, tells his daughter to turn down the music a little bit. One of the father's business partners says, "Oh, isn't she sweet!" They return to the den. Minutes later, Mary turns up the volume on the stereo to an even louder level.

   _____

   _____

   _____

   _____

   _____

   _____

   _____

Checking
Your Progress

2. True or False

   _____ a. Gestures, facial expressions, and other forms of body language all give meaning to what you communicate.

   _____ b. Nonverbal communication supplements verbal communication.

   _____ c. Gestures include the moving of the hands, head, or other parts of the body while speaking.

   _____ d. Nonverbal cues only add confusion to the process of discipline.

   _____ e. Nonverbal praise is vital to behavior management because a wink or a smile communicates your caring and support for a child's appropriate behaviors.

   _____ f. Nonverbal communication is effective only when it is used in place of verbal language.

   _____ g. It is important to be naturally expressive with all your children, hearing and nonhearing alike.

   _____ h. Nonverbal communication provides clarity to what you say or do, and also aids in developing your consistency as a behavior manager.

CHAPTER NINE

Putting It All Together

INTRODUCTION

You have now reached the final chapters of this book. Thus far, we have discussed feelings about hearing impairment, dealing with those feelings, the behavior of hearing-impaired children, and how to handle misbehavior. We have looked at the importance of nonverbal communication in our interactions with other human beings. A great deal of information has been presented. You may not retain all the information discussed, but you can refer back to the information and use it as general guidelines for future interactions with your child.

In this chapter, we will review several points and help you apply these points specifically to enhance the interactions between you and your child. We will give you guidelines to help you develop a personal plan of action—a plan for working with your behavior and the behavior of your hearing-impaired child.

This chapter does not follow the same format as the previous chapters. It is now time to put the information you have read to use—to put it all together.

In order to get the most from this chapter, you must decide where to begin. Use specific information relative to your own family. For example, perhaps you suspect that your feelings are interfering with how effectively you handle your child's behavior. Maybe you would profit from reviewing the section on recognizing your feelings, paying close attention to outlining how to cope and work with your feelings.

If you have a child with a specific problem behavior, you may want to look closely at the section involving the use of the A-B-C pattern. If you are interested in developing basic rules for your household that are consistent and clearly understood, then concentrate on the area of this chapter that illustrates how general rules are developed.

You have mastered valuable information about you and your hearing-impaired child while reading this book. It is now time to put that knowledge to use. At the end of this chapter, there are worksheets to assist you in those areas where you have the greatest need.

Problem Solving

You can treat improving the interactions within your family as a problem-solving situation. Problem solving involves five steps: (1) identify the problem area; (2) determine your goal or what you want to happen; (3) decide what is stopping you from getting to that goal; (4) consider strategies needed to get you to your goal; and (5) implement a plan and evaluate its effectiveness.

> *You have mastered valuable information about you and your hearing-impaired child while reading this book.*

Let us look at an example illustrating the use of problem-solving techniques with your hearing-impaired child: Suppose your child does not comply with your requests. Your goal is to get your child to obey when you make requests; however, your emotions may be an obstacle that prevents you from achieving your goal. A strategy for overcoming this obstacle would be to discuss what you want done at a time when you are calm. You can evaluate the effectiveness of this strategy by measuring how often your child follows your directions when you present them in a calm manner.

The personal plan you develop should follow this general problem-solving approach. In the future, you can use the approach as a step-by-step strategy to solve a variety of problems. The three worksheets that follow present information on the three problem areas introduced throughout this book: dealing with strong feelings, setting limits, and implementing behavior-management plans. You can use one or all three worksheets depending on your needs. Before you begin to develop your personal plan, we will discuss one last area.

An important part of the problem-solving approach is evaluating your strategy.

Evaluation

An important part of the problem-solving approach is evaluating your strategy. Any time you decide on a problem-solving strategy, you need to determine if the strategy works. One way to make this determination is to ask yourself if you feel better about what is happening, or if the situation is better as a result of what you have done. You can also use the A-B-C pattern to evaluate the success of this strategy. By measuring your child's behavior before, during, and after the implementation of your plan, you can determine if your method is succeeding. If the information you receive from your charts, graphs, and your feelings indicate your plan is not successful, you must revise your strategy. This is a crucial part of solving problems. Let us look at the problem-solving method again to emphasize how important evaluation is in determining its success. The following example illustrates this point.

Example of Problem Solving:

1. Problem: Billy throws a tantrum when asked to put away his toys.

2. Goal: To stop Billy's tantrum behaviors.

3. Obstacles: When Billy throws a tantrum, I give in. I get so angry I lose control.

4. Strategy: Use the A-B-C pattern to help stop tantrum behaviors.

A Antecedent	B Behavior	C Consequences
Billy is in the playroom. Billy is told to put away his toys.	Billy throws a tantrum.	Billy's play period is taken away.

5. Evaluation: I measured Billy's behavior. Tantrum behaviors did not decrease after one week. I need to change my strategy or part of my strategy. I will change the consequences to two minutes in time-out room. I will implement my strategy as soon as possible. I will reevaluate this new strategy after one week.

Dealing with Your Feelings

1. Before you work on behavior, either your own or your child's, you need to be aware of your feelings. Your feelings are reactions to situations of the past, present, or what you believe may occur in the future. Feelings may stem from painful experiences that happened years ago or from present experiences, such as dealing with the behavior of your hearing-impaired child. The following statements address aspects about your feelings related to your child's hearing loss. Becoming aware of your feelings and controlling them will help you make better decisions.

Check those statements that apply to your feelings about the diagnosis of your child's hearing loss.

a. _____ I have strong feelings about my child's hearing impairment.

b. _____ I wish over and over again that my child could hear normally.

c. _____ Many times I still feel angry about those days when my child was first being diagnosed as having a hearing loss.

d. _____ I get upset about the way the doctors, audiologists, and other medical staff handled the situation.

e. _____ I am frustrated over the entire situation in dealing with my child's hearing-impaired condition.

f. _____ List any other feelings you may have regarding the diagnosis of your child's hearing loss:

_____

_____

_____

_____

_____

_____

The above list of statements makes explicit certain feelings you may have about the diagnosis of your child's hearing impairment. If you checked one or more of the statements or added comments concerning your feelings, it is important not to ignore that these feelings exist. Dealing with the feelings can help you overcome them and help you cope with your life as it has changed as a result of having a child with a hearing loss. Continue with the next series of statements and develop your plan for working to cope with the feelings that you are experiencing.

2. Dealing with hearing loss on a daily basis, I find that

Check those that apply.

a. _____ I am frightened when I think of what will happen to my child in the world.

b. _____ I get upset when I see hearing children playing or working together.

c. _____ Sometimes I get angry and upset when trying to discipline my child because of our communication problem.

d. _____ I am tired of trying to communicate with my child each day. We never seem to get anywhere.

e. _____ I often feel sad when my child becomes frustrated and cannot understand because of the communication problems.

f. _____ At times I feel overwhelmed because of the responsibility of taking care of my family and looking after the needs of my hearing-impaired child.

g. _____ List any other feelings that come up because of your child's hearing loss:

_____

_____

_____

_____

Your response to the previous statements describe feelings that are common. Parents with hearing-impaired children report having these same feelings from time to time. Do not ignore them. Use the following guide to help develop a plan to deal with some of the feelings you have because of the diagnosis of your child's hearing loss or what the hearing impairment means to you and your family.

A Plan for Dealing with Feelings

3. List some of your feelings that frequently occur.

Example: Sadness about my child's hearing loss—Why did this happen?

_____

Be specific.

_____

_____

_____

4. List ways you have used to deal with your feelings about the diagnosis of your child's hearing loss or what the hearing impairment means to you and your family.

    Example: When feeling depressed about how the hearing impairment affects my family, I watch television, sleep, or do work around the house.

List coping strategies.

_____

_____

_____

_____

_____

_____

5. Have these ways of coping worked? Yes ___ No ___
   If no, list alternative ways to deal with your feelings.

    Example: When I feel depressed, I usually watch television and forget about it. (The depression does not lessen. Feeling: depression. Alternative ways of coping: talk to my close friend about feelings, talk to my spouse, or talk to another parent of a hearing-impaired child.)

State feeling and way of coping.

_____

_____

_____

_____

_____

6. Fill in the blank: I get very upset about my hearing-impaired child's behavior when _____.

    Example: my child closes his eyes when I am talking to him.

Describe the specific situations when you have strong feelings.

_____

_____

_____

_____

_____

_____

7. Describe how you typically deal with your strong feelings.

Example: When my child looks away when I talk to him, I hold his face until he looks at me.

_____

_____

_____

_____

_____

_____

_____

_____

Describe ways of coping.

8. Do these ways of coping work? Yes ___ No ___.
    If no, list alternative ways to deal with your feelings:

Example: When my child misbehaves and I am feeling very angry, I can wait until I am calm before I try to communicate with my son.

_____

_____

_____

_____

_____

_____

_____

Think about alternate strategies.

Continue to evaluate whether the ways you cope work in helping you deal with your feelings.

Worksheet 2

Developing Rules

Perhaps you need to develop a list of clear and consistent rules. The following plan will help you in preparing or improving a rule system in your home.

Date:_____

1. What general rules do you want your child to obey at home?

   Example: Use polite language in the home.

> *Be specific about behaviors wanted and state rules in the positive.*

   a. _____

   b. _____

   c. _____

   d. _____

   e. _____

2. What will you do the first time your child breaks these main rules?

   Example: Remind child about the rule, give a warning, etc.

   a. _____

   b. _____

   c. _____

   d. _____

   e. _____

3. What will you do the second time your child breaks the main rules?

   Example: Take away privileges, make the child stay inside the house for a half hour, etc.

   a. _____

   b. _____

   c. _____

   d. _____

   e. _____

You and Your Hearing-Impaired Child

4. How will you reward your child for following your main rules? Use the space provided below to list your thoughts concerning use of rewards. (See Appendix 1 for ideas on reinforcement.)

   Example: The child will be verbally praised throughout the day and will earn an extra privilege (e.g., spend an extra half hour at the park).

_____

_____

_____

_____

_____

_____

_____

_____

_____

> *Remember to reward appropriate behavior.*

5. What rules do you need to set for specific times of the day? (State rules in a positive way.)

> *The word __no__ should not appear.*

Play Period

a. _____

b. _____

c. _____

Dinner Time

a. _____

b. _____

c. _____

Bed Time

a. _____

b. _____

c. _____

Other (Specify)

a. _____

b. _____

c. _____

6. What will you do the first time your child breaks these specific rules?

> Example: Remind them about the rule, give a warning, etc.

Play Period

a. _____

b. _____

c. _____

Bed Time

a. _____

b. _____

c. _____

Dinner Time

a. _____

b. _____

c. _____

Other (Specify)

a. _____

b. _____

c. _____

7. What will you do the second time your child breaks a specific rule?

> Example: Take away privileges; child loses portion of playtime.

Play Period

a. _____

b. _____

c. _____

Bed Time

a. _____

b. _____

c. _____

Dinner Time

a. _____

b. _____

c. _____

Other (Specify)

a. _____

b. _____

c. _____

8. What will you do when your child follows the specific rules in your home? (See Appendix 1 for ideas.)

_____

_____

_____

_____

_____

_____

| *Describe positive reinforcers.* |

Evaluation of Plan

9. Did you generally respond to your child in the way you wanted?

   Yes _____   No _____

10. Did you clearly communicate the rules to your child?

    Yes _____   No _____

11. Did you follow up the rule with the appropriate consequence consistently (every time) when your child broke the rule?

    Yes _____   No _____

12. Are your set consequences (negative and positive) helping your child follow the rules?

    Yes _____   No _____

13. Review your overall plan—do you need to change all or part of your plan?

    Yes _____   No _____

_____

_____

_____

_____

_____

| *Write your comments here.* |

Worksheet 3

A Plan for Behavior Management

Date:_____

1. Which two specific behavior(s) do you believe your child must change or stop?

   a. _____

   b. _____

2. Look at the behaviors you just listed above in their settings (antecedents) and determine what happens after these behaviors occur (consequences). Write the antecedents, behaviors, and consequences in the chart below.

A Antecedent	B Behavior	C Consequences

3. Choose one of the behaviors listed above. Measure the behavior over time (a week or two is suggested) before you begin your behavior management program. Use the behavior chart on the next page.

Behavior:				Period of Observation:	_____ Throughout Day _____ Part of Day From _____ to _____ (specify time)			
Sunday	Monday	Tuesday	Wednesday	Thursday	Friday	Saturday	Total	Dates

4. Which disciplinary consequences will you use when the misbehavior occurs? For example, taking away a privilege (television, friends over, allowance); ignoring; time out; etc.

_____

_____

_____

_____

_____

_____

5. Which positive consequences will you use when you reinforce appropriate behavior? (See the reinforcement chart in Appendix 1.)

_____

_____

List positive reinforcers.

_____

_____

_____

_____

_____

_____

_____

6. Continue to measure the behavior using the behavior chart below (transfer the information you gathered on page 101). Graph the results to see if your program is working. Refer to chapter six to review methods of measuring, charting, and graphing the frequency or duration of behaviors. (Extra behavior charts and graphs are located in Appendix 2. Remember, keep measuring the behavior throughout the program.)

Behavior:								
Period of Observation: _____ Throughout Day _____ Part of Day From _____ to _____ (specify time)								
Sunday	Monday	Tuesday	Wednesday	Thursday	Friday	Saturday	Total	Dates

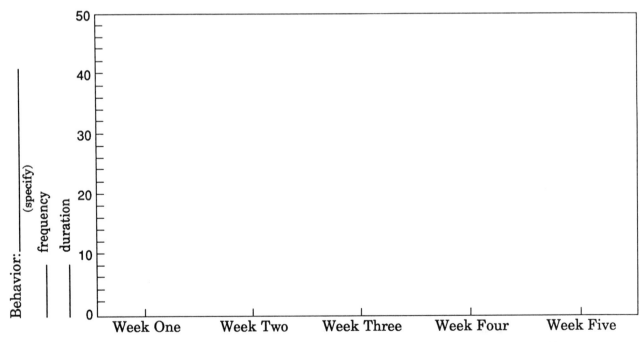

Note: Indicate the beginning of your behavior change program with a broken vertical line.

7. Evaluate your plan to see if the misbehavior has decreased. By reviewing your graphs and by the way you generally feel about the situation, you can determine whether your plan is working. If it is not working, go back to your A-B-C patterns and see what antecedents and consequences need to be changed. It may be necessary to analyze one or several A-B-C patterns concerning your child's behaviors before you discover the antecedents or consequences that need to be changed. After you make changes in your plan, continue to measure the behavior.

Consider these thoughts: Do you clearly explain the consequences to your child? Are you consistent in giving your consequences? Do you carefully consider how the hearing-impaired condition may affect the consequences and antecedents involved in your child's behavior? Is your new plan working?

Write your comments here.

CHAPTER TEN

Meeting Your Needs

INTRODUCTION

Being a parent of a hearing-impaired child produces many concerns and questions about the future. What effect will hearing impairment have on your child's life? How will this disability influence and change your life and the development of your family? Will your child be able to lead a "normal" life? Can your child find happiness? How can you gather more information about the areas new to you concerning hearing impairment?

Throughout this book, we have concentrated on learning more about your feelings, your behavior, your child's behavior, behavior management, and developing ways of coping with your situation. Gathering information about hearing impairment and how it affects your child and your life is one way of coping. This strategy enables you to begin understanding hearing impairment and its implications and helps you develop expectations for you and your child.

In this chapter we examine several areas deemed important in meeting the needs of hearing-impaired children: language development, choice of communication and amplification, educational placement, and the deaf culture. The information provided in this chapter may also help you locate the specific information you need to cope with many unanswered questions. Each area is examined briefly. Sources relative to each area are provided in chapter eleven. These resources and the list of Suggested Reading beginning on page 120 can be helpful in your quest for better understanding of the hearing-impaired condition.

Language Development

Hearing-impaired youngsters nearly always experience language delays or deficits (Schlesinger, 1985). Many different factors can influence a hearing-impaired child's language development. Onset of hearing loss, amount of residual hearing, hearing status of parent, etc. are but a few of these factors. Like all children, hearing-impaired children have a capacity for language (Mindel & Vernon, 1987). The problem is not that hearing-impaired children are being deprived of sounds, as much as they are being deprived of language (Meadow, 1980). Hearing-impaired children have difficulty communicating wants, needs, thoughts, and feelings, and you face this difficulty with them. In order for language to develop, you must actively seek out interactions with your hearing-impaired child. These interactions can occur during such routines as bedtime, playtime, dinner, games, and getting ready for school.

In order for language to develop, you must actively seek out interactions with your hearing-impaired child.

You must be actively involved in providing guidance to help your hearing-impaired child refer to the world in a meaningful way. The development of effective language is connected to the availability of interaction through experiences provided (Heimgartner, 1982).

Communication Choices

Good communication involves much more than just an exchange of words. Communication implies an interaction that involves sharing. It is important that a family with a hearing-impaired member use an easy, fluent system of communication (Quigley & Kretschmer, 1982). There exists little disagreement about the need for an easy, fluent communication system; the disagreement comes in choosing the types of communication methods and language to be used.

The best method of communication for hearing-impaired children has been hotly debated for years. The conflict has focused on the use of spoken language vs. sign language (Meadow, 1980). The choice of the method of communication used with your child is yours and yours alone. Your choice should be made after carefully considering what is best for your child and for your family.

The following paragraphs contain information about a few of the options available to parents regarding their choice for communication method.

Individuals promoting the oral/aural communication method stress the use of speech, hearing aids, voice, and speechreading skills. Children using this method are discouraged from relying on visual cues except those involved with lip movements used in speech. Proponents of this method promote the teaching of oral communication skills and the training of residual hearing to facilitate language and speech development (Becker, 1981). The goal of this method is to provide the child with oral skills that will enable him or her to function in a hearing society.

The Oral Method

Individuals promoting the manual communication method stress the use of gestures and sign language as the primary mode of communication for hearing-impaired children. Children using this visual method use signs and fingerspelling to communicate their ideas. The proponents of this method presume that the use of a manual means of communication such as signs is effective in teaching language to hearing-impaired children. They believe that the knowledge and understanding of language is more important than the ability to speak intelligibly (Mindel & Vernon, 1987). The supporters of the manual method also believe that hearing-impaired children have a better chance of developing social and language skills via sign language (Becker, 1981).

The Manual Method

Individuals promoting the simultaneous method stress the use of speech produced simultaneously with manual gestures that represent the spoken language. Proponents of this method assume that it is possible to represent the spoken language visually. Also, they believe that a hearing-impaired child can learn language in the same fashion

Simultaneous Method

> *The choice of communication method should not be delayed for too long after the child is diagnosed as hearing-impaired.*

as a hearing child—through the use of spoken and visual forms of communication (Mindel & Vernon, 1987). Proponents of this method emphasize that providing both the oral and signing options simultaneously allows the child to learn language in a way best suited to his or her needs while developing communication skills to function in the hearing world (Mindel & Vernon, 1987; Schlesinger & Meadow, 1972).

Total communication, which is an application of the simultaneous method, promotes the use of all possible methods of communication (such as listening, speechreading, signing, etc.) to assist hearing-impaired children in acquiring language and understanding its use. Total communication is a "philosophy requiring the incorporation of appropriate aural, manual, and oral modes of communication in order to ensure effective communication with and among hearing-impaired persons" (Conference of Executives of American Schools for the Deaf, 1976, p. 358).

Parents of hearing-impaired children need to consider all the approaches to communication. No one method is right for all hearing-impaired children and their families. Each family must choose the modes and approaches suited to its needs. Most important, the method chosen must be appropriate for your child's needs. For example, if your child has enough residual hearing that he or she could develop speech, you may decide to choose a strictly oral approach. On the other hand, if your child lacks all auditory input even with hearing aids, then you might decide on an approach using manual means of communicating (Boothroyd, 1982).

Even though no one correct method exists for all children and their families, you must make a choice early in your child's life. The choice of communication method (oral, manual, or simultaneous) should not be delayed for too long after the child is diagnosed as hearing-impaired. Consistent use of one method will enable your child to begin to acquire language and eventually become an active member of your family. Some professionals believe hearing aids should be used as soon as possible, regardless of the option chosen. Once you have obtained the aids, you can continue to investigate your options for communication (Ling, 1984). Take the time to explore your options thoroughly by gathering information from reading material, professionals (such as teachers, doctors, and counselors), other parents of hearing-impaired children, and hearing-impaired adults. Gathering information from a variety of sources will help make your options clear and help you make an informed choice.

In all cases and in all choices made, you need to be motivated and willing to learn communication methods that are different than those you are accustomed to. This will give your hearing-impaired child access to clear and understandable means of communication in which you and your child become actively involved.

Hearing Aids

The use of hearing aids is considered by many as vital in the educating and socializing of hearing-impaired children. Relatives or friends often believe that hearing-impaired children can become hearing as soon as they are fitted with hearing aids (Meadow, 1980). But hearing aids are not a substitute for hearing; nothing can substitute for your child's ability to hear. A hearing aid only makes sounds louder; it does not restore hearing (Rodda & Grove, 1987). Most hearing-impaired children, however, have some residual hearing that may be amplified (Luterman, 1986).

> *A hearing aid only makes sounds louder; it does not restore hearing.*

The type of hearing loss your child has will determine how the hearing aid can help. In one case, a hearing aid will enable a child to hear only very loud sounds. In another case, a hearing aid may permit words or phrases to be heard. The type of hearing loss will determine which hearing aid is best for your child and what sounds will be made louder.

The hearing aid is basically a microphone, an amplifier, and an ear mold that must be properly placed in the ear. Hearing aids exist in a variety of shapes and sizes. These range from a radio-transmission system that is typically used in the classroom and is the size of a small box to a small aid that is worn inside the ear (Rodda & Grove, 1987).

A hearing aid will aid a child's hearing only if it is used as a consistent and integral part of the child's life. If used haphazardly or inconsistently, the aid may add confusion since what is picked up from the environment may change from day to day.

Educational Placement

The type of school environment has been a major issue in educating hearing-impaired children. It has historically been related to issues in communication (Quigley & Kretschmer, 1982). For example, many times parents choose the education placement for their child based on the type of communication method used in the home. Specifically, if you decide on an oral approach to communication, you might seek out a school placement that uses an oral approach for intervention. In

> *You have a choice in school programs for your child.*

addition to having a variety of educational placements, depending on the communication method you choose, you also have a choice in school programs for your child.

Residential Schools

These schools can be found in the public and private sectors. A residential school provides both educational and living facilities for hearing-impaired students, with few or no provisions for integration with hearing students (Quigley & Kretschmer, 1982). In most programs the children spend weekends at home with their families. These schools offer a variety of educational, social, and recreational programs for hearing-impaired children.

Day-School Programs

These programs can also be found in the public and private sectors. Day schools are usually located in large populated areas. Students go to school with hearing-impaired students only. Students attend the school during regular daytime hours and return home after program hours.

Day Classes

Day classes are usually located in a school for the general population and provide some degree of integration and mainstreaming of hearing-impaired students with normal-hearing students (Quigley & Kretschmer, 1982). The classes are usually self-contained, and all students in the class are hearing-impaired. Children can participate in a variety of activities with normal-hearing peers such as lunch, physical education, and certain academic subjects.

Mainstreaming Programs

Mainstreaming programs involve placing the hearing-impaired child in a classroom with normal-hearing children. In this type of program it is important to consider the availability of support services for the hearing-impaired child, such as interpreters, tutors, visual aids, etc. You must ensure that your mainstreamed child is having his or her educational needs met appropriately.

The area in which you live may have an impact on your choice of educational placements or may limit the options available to you. A family living in a heavily populated metropolitan area may have access to many services, but a family living in a more scarcely populated area may have far fewer educational options. The relatively low incidence of hearing impairment in the population suggests that only those school systems that serve a large population will be able to provide enough support services to meet the needs of hearing-impaired children adequately. Budget cuts and funding constraints will also have effects on the amount of programming and services available. You need to be alert to these shifts of funding or attitudes concerning the provision of services in order to make informed decisions (Davis, 1986).

The right school for a hearing-impaired child varies from child to child, family to family, area to area (McArthur, 1982). You need to undertake an objective evaluation to determine the best placement for your child. Keep in mind that you need not make any decision for your hearing-impaired child alone. Professionals, other parents of hearing-impaired children, and hearing-impaired adults can offer information that will aid you in your decision making.

Culture

The deaf community is in itself a miniature society. It includes a cross-section of people with differing hearing losses, physical builds, races, religions, intelligence, interests, and values (Rosen, 1986). The common trait among all is the inability to hear. Everyone in this world needs to belong. Hearing-impaired people are no different. Many hearing-impaired individuals function as outsiders in a hearing world. Oftentimes they find themselves treated as minorities similar to other groups (e.g., blacks, Jews, gays, etc.).

Deaf culture binds the community together—a shared language (sign language), interests, and experiences determine this culture. Since the problem in dealing with the hearing world is communication, hearing-impaired persons tend to socialize together more than do persons with other disabilities. A knowledge of deaf culture is vital to hearing-impaired children so they can know and understand that culture. Children need to have hearing-impaired role models to help them develop a healthy self-image (Rodda & Grove, 1987). It is also helpful for the parents of hearing-impaired children to meet hearing-impaired adults. This can help you see that hearing-impaired individuals can be productive, successful, contributing individuals in their own community as well as in the larger society.

> *Children need to have hearing-impaired role models to help them develop a healthy self-image.*

CHAPTER ELEVEN

Conclusion

Obtaining information is helpful whether you have just discovered your child's hearing loss or you have had years of experience in dealing with it.

Congratulations! You have completed this book in an effort to gain a better understanding of yourself and your hearing-impaired child. By reading the material presented in this book and completing the activities offered, you have taken an opportunity to learn more about hearing loss and its impact on your family. You have examined your feelings about hearing impairment, your behavior and your child's behavior, and the interactions between you. In doing so, you have taken a risk to grow as a person and most especially as a parent of a hearing-impaired child. Looking within yourself is difficult at times, but an important part of growing and understanding is being aware of how your feelings and behavior influence you and your interactions with others.

If the information presented in this book has been difficult for you or has helped bring about unwanted feelings, do not be discouraged. You have made a step toward obtaining information about hearing loss in relation to your family.

Gathering information is an important part of coping. Obtaining information is helpful whether you have just discovered your child's hearing loss or you have had years of experience in dealing with it. In either case, this book has given you information you can use in the future. This book was designed to reach a variety of parents with hearing-impaired children of differing ages. You can use this book again and again depending on your specific needs throughout your development as a parent and your child's growing years. You may find that as your child matures you will react differently to the material in this book. Or your thoughts and ideas concerning the activities in each chapter may change.

In addition to using this book as a reference guide as your child matures, you may also review it based upon *your* individual needs. You can review or redo particular chapters or combinations of chapters as a source of information. For example, if you experience difficulty in dealing with your feelings or would like to gain a better understanding of feelings related to deafness, you could re-read chapters two and three and complete worksheets 1 and 2 in chapter nine. Or, perhaps you would like to gain more of an understanding about "normal" child behavior at certain age levels and how hearing loss influences behavior and development. A review of chapter four may be beneficial for this purpose. If you would like to place general limits on your child's behavior or develop specific programs for behavior change in your hearing-impaired child, you can refer to chapters five, six, and seven. Additional resources for parents of hearing-impaired children are listed in this chapter, and a list of suggested readings begins on page 120.

   I hope that this book was helpful to you and will be helpful to others involved with the care and development of hearing-impaired children. Since you have read this book, you are in a unique position to offer your opinions about how this book can be developed to better meet your needs and the needs of other parents of hearing-impaired children. You may have ideas, thoughts, or suggestions about how to make the book more useful to you and others like yourself. Please share these thoughts with me. Your statements will be kept in strict confidence. If you have such comments, please complete the form on page 129 and mail it to the address listed on the form.

   I hope that this book has been helpful to you and in some way has touched your life. Without a doubt, gathering the information in writing this book, especially my contact with parents of hearing-impaired children and professionals who work with hearing-impaired children has touched, if not changed, a part of me. Thank you.

Organizations and Services

American Deafness and Rehabilitation Association
PO Box 55369
Little Rock, AR 72225
(501) 375-6643 Voice/TDD

Culture

GLAD: Greater Los Angeles Council on Deafness, Inc.
616 South Westmoreland Avenue
Los Angeles, CA 90005
(213) 383-2220 Voice/TDD

Self-Help for Hard of Hearing People, Inc. (SHHH)
7800 Wisconsin Avenue
Bethesda, MD 20814
(301) 657-2248 Voice
(301) 657-2249 TDD

American Organization for the Education of the Hearing-Impaired
3417 Volta Place, NW
Washington, DC 20007
(202) 337-5220 Voice/TDD

Educational Placement

The Conference of Educational Administrators Serving the Deaf
The American School for the Deaf
139 N. Main Street
West Hartford, CT 06107
(203) 727-1300 Voice/TDD

The Convention of American Instructors of the Deaf
PO Box 2163
Columbia, MD 21045
(301) 461-9988 Voice/TDD

The Council for Exceptional Children
1920 Association Drive
Reston, VA 22091
(800) 336-3728 Voice/TDD
(703) 620-3660

Hearing Aids

Alexander Graham Bell Association for the Deaf
3417 Volta Place, NW
Washington, DC 20007
(202) 337-5220 Voice/TDD

Com-Tek
375 West Lemel Circle
Salt Lake City, UT 84115
(415) 383-4000

Gallaudet University Audiology Department
800 Florida Avenue, NE
Washington, DC 20002
(202) 651-5358 Voice/TDD

National Hearing Aid Society
20361 Middlebelt Road
Livonia, MI 48152
(313) 478-2610 Voice/TDD
(800) 521-5248 Hearing Aid Helpline

National Technical Institute for the Deaf
PO Box 9887
Rochester, NY 14623
(716) 475-6824 Voice/TDD

Phonic Ear Inc.
250 Camino Alto
Mill Valley, CA 94941
(415) 383-4000

Telex Communications, Inc.
9600 Aldrich Avenue South
Minneapolis, MN 55420
(612) 884-7430

Miscellaneous Resources

Alexander Graham Bell Association for the Deaf
3417 Volta Place, NW
Washington, DC 20007
(202) 337-5220 Voice/TDD

American Society for Deaf Children
814 Thayer Avenue
Silver Spring, MD 20910
(301) 585-5400 Voice/TDD

American Speech-Language-Hearing Association
10801 Rockville Pike
Rockville, MD 20852
(301) 897-5700 Voice/TDD

Better Hearing Institute
PO Box 1840
Washington, DC 20013
(703) 642-0580
(800) EAR-WELL

Captioned Films for the Deaf
Modern Talking Pictures Services, Inc.
5000 Park Street North
St. Petersburg, FL 33709
(800) 237-6213 Voice/TDD

Council for Exceptional Children
1920 Association Drive
Reston, VA 22091
(800) 336-3728 Voice/TDD
(703) 620-3660

Deafness and Communication Disorders Branch
Rehabilitation Services Administration
Department of Education
330 C Street, SW Room 3316
Washington, DC 20201
(202) 732-1401 Voice
(202) 732-1298 TDD

Deafpride, Inc.
1350 Potomac Avenue, SE
Washington, DC 20003
(202) 675-6700 Voice/TDD

Deaf Counseling, Advocacy, and Referral Agency (DCARA)
125 Parott Street
San Leandro, CA 94577
(415) 895-2432 Voice/TDD

Deaf Counseling, Advocacy, and Referral Agency (DCARA) Bookstore
Town Fair Shopping Center
39138 State Street
Fremont, CA 94538
(415) 796-7660 Voice
(415) 796-7661 TDD

Gallaudet University
800 Florida Avenue, NE
Washington, DC 20002
(202) 651-5000 Voice/TDD
(800) 672-6720 Voice/TDD

Miscellaneous Resources

Greater Los Angeles Council on Deafness, Inc. (GLAD) Bookstore
616 South Westmoreland Avenue
Los Angeles, CA 90005
(213) 383-2220 Voice/TDD

House Ear Institute
256 South Lake
Los Angeles, CA 90057
(213) 483-4431 Voice
(213) 484-2642 TDD

John Tracy Clinic
806 West Adams Boulevard
Los Angeles, CA 90007
(213) 748-5481 Voice
(213) 747-2924 TDD
(800) 522-4582

Modern Signs Press
PO Box 1181
Los Alamitos, CA 90720

National Association for Hearing and Speech Action
10801 Rockville Pike
Rockville, MD 20852
(301) 897-8682 Voice/TDD
(800) 638-TALK Voice/TDD

National Association of the Deaf
814 Thayer Avenue
Silver Spring, MD 20910
(301) 587-1788 Voice/TDD

National Center for Law and the Deaf
Gallaudet University
800 Florida Avenue, NE
Washington, DC 20002
(202) 651-5373 Voice/TDD

National Hearing Association
1010 Jorie Boulevard, #308
Oak Brook, IL 60521
(312) 323-7200

National Information Center for Handicapped Children and Youth
PO Box 1492
Washington, DC 20013
(702) 522-3332

National Information Center on Deafness
Gallaudet University
800 Florida Avenue, NE
Washington, DC 20002
(202) 651-5051 Voice, X5052 TDD
(800) 672-6720 X5051 Voice, X5052 TDD

National Rehabilitation Information Center (NARIC)
Catholic University of America
4407 Eighth Street, NE
Washington, DC 20017
(202) 635-5826 Voice/TDD
(800) 346-2742 Voice/TDD

National Technical Institute for the Deaf
Rochester Institute of Technology
One Lomb Memorial Drive
PO Box 9887
Rochester, NY 14623
(716) 475-6400 Voice
(716) 475-2181 TDD

Parent to Parent
256 South Lake Street
Los Angeles, CA 90057
(213) 483-4431 Voice
(213) 484-2642 TDD

Registry of Interpreters for the Deaf, Inc.
One Metro Square
51 Monroe Street, Suite 1107
Rockville, MD 20850
(301) 279-0555 Voice/TDD
(301) 279-6773

Special Office for Materials Distribution
Indiana University Audio-Visual Center
(This Center distributes educational captioned films and other
teaching aids for the hearing-impaired.)
Bloomington, IN 47401

Telecommunications for the Deaf, Inc.
814 Thayer Avenue
Silver Spring, MD 20910
(301) 589-3006 Voice/TDD

The National Theatre of the Deaf
The Hazel E. Stark Center
Chester, CT 06412
(203) 526-4971 Voice
(203) 526-4974 TDD

TRIPOD
955 North Alfred Street
Los Angeles, CA 90069
(213) 656-4904 Voice/TDD
National Helpline: The Grapevine
California: (800) 346-8888
Outside California: (800) 352-8888

Clearinghouse on the Handicapped
Switzer Building, Room 3132
Washington, DC 20202
(202) 732-1245

Pamphlets, Brochures, and Activity Kits

Legal Rights Kit
Alexander Graham Bell Association for the Deaf
3417 Volta Place, NW
Washington, DC 20007

Mainstreaming Kit
Alexander Graham Bell Association for the Deaf
3417 Volta Place, NW
Washington, DC 20007

Resource Kit
American Society for Deaf Children
814 Thayer Avenue
Silver Spring, MD 20910

Pamphlets available from:
The Convention of American Instructors of the Deaf
P.O. Box 2163
Columbia, MD 21045

The Rights of Parents
The National Committee for Citizens in Education
10840 Little Patuxent Parkway, Suite 301
Columbia, MD 21044

Pamphlets on hearing aid use are available from:
Alexander Graham Bell Association for the Deaf
3417 Volta Place, NW
Washington, DC 20007

Language Motivating Experiences for Young Children (Activity kit)
by R. C. Engel
Educational Toys & Supplies
6416 Van Nuys Boulevard
Van Nuys, CA 91401

Visually Cued Language Cards
by R. Foster and J.J. Giddan
Consulting Psychologists Press
577 College Avenue
Palo Alto, CA 94306

References

Algozzine, R., Schmid, R., & Mercer, D. C. (1981). *Childhood behavior disorders: Applied research and educational practice.* Rockville, MD: Aspen Systems.

Allen, J. C., & Allen, M. L. (1979). Discovering and accepting hearing-impairment: Initial reactions of parents. *The Volta Review, 81,* 279–285.

Baker, B. L., Brightman, A. J., Heifetz, L. J., & Murphy, D. M. (1976). *Behavior problems.* Champaign, IL: Research Press.

Becker, S. (1981). Counseling the families of deaf children: A mental health worker speaks out. *Journal of Rehabilitation of the Deaf, 15,* 10–15.

Belcastro, F. (1979). Use of behavior modification with hearing-impaired subjects. *American Annals of the Deaf, 124,* 820–823.

Bolton, B. (1976). *Psychology of deafness for rehabilitation counselors.* Baltimore, MD: University Park Press.

Boothroyd, A. (1982). *Hearing-impairments in young children.* Englewood Cliffs, NJ: Prentice-Hall.

Brenner, B. (1983). *Love and discipline.* New York: Ballantine Books.

Brown, S. C. (1986). Etiological trends, characteristics, and distributions. In A. N. Schildroth and M. A. Karcher (Eds.), *Deaf children in America* (pp. 33–54). San Diego, CA: College Hill Press.

Canter, L., & Canter, M. (1985). *Lee Canter's assertive discipline for parents* (rev. ed.). Santa Monica, CA: Canter.

Champ-Wilson, A. (1982). Successful parenting: Fact or fiction. In *Parent education resource manual* (pp. 191–196). Washington, DC: Gallaudet University.

Conference of Executives of American Schools for the Deaf. (1976). Total communication definition adopted. *American Annals of the Deaf, 121,* 358.

Correspondence course for parents of young deaf children. (1983). (Available from John Tracy Clinic, 806 West Adams Blvd., Los Angeles, CA 90007).

Davis, F. (1973). *Inside intuition: What we know about nonverbal communication,* New York: McGraw-Hill.

Davis, J. (1986). Academic placement in perspective. In D. M. Luterman (Ed.), *Deafness in perspective* (pp. 205–224). San Diego, CA: College Hill Press.

Deyo, D., & Gelzer, L. (1987). *When a hearing loss is diagnosed.* (Pamphlet available from the National Information Center on Deafness, Gallaudet University, 800 Florida Ave., NE, Washington, DC 20002).

Dinkmeyer, D., & McKay, G. D. (1976). *Systematic training for effective parenting: Parent's handbook.* Circle Pines, MN: American Guidance Service.

Gesell, A., Ilg, F. L., & Bates-Ames, L. (1977). *The child from five to ten* (rev. ed.). New York: Harper & Row.

Goldberg, H. K. (1979). Hearing-impairment: A family crisis. *Social Work in Health Care, 5,* 33–40.

Green, R. R. (1971, Winter). Pointers for parents: The hearing-impaired child at home. *Highlights,* 5–7.

Gregory, S. (1976). *The deaf child and his family.* New York: Wiley.

Heimgartner, N. L. (1982). *Behavioral traits of deaf children.* Springfield, IL: Charles C. Thomas.

Herbert, M. (1981). *Behavioral treatment of problem children: A practice manual.* New York: Academic Press.

Hubler, S. (Ed.). (1983). *When your perfect child is deaf.* A discussion guide to accompany the film: "My perfect child is deaf." (Available from The House Ear Institute, Los Angeles, CA 90057)

Kazdin, A. E. (1984). *Behavior modification in applied settings.* Homewood, IL: Dorsey Press.

Kretschmer, R. R. (Ed.). (1979). Parenting a hearing-impaired child: An interview with Ken Moses. *The Volta Review, 81,* 73–80.

Kretschmer, R. R., & Kretschmer, L. (1986). Language in perspective. In D.M. Luterman (Ed.), *Deafness in perspective* (pp. 131–166). San Diego, CA: College Hill Press.

Liben, L. S. (1978). *Deaf children: Developmental perspectives.* New York: Academic Press.

Ling, D. (1984). *Early intervention for hearing-impaired children: Total communication options.* San Diego, CA: College Hill Press.

Luterman, D. M. (1986). *Deafness in perspective.* San Diego, CA: College Hill Press.

McArthur, S. H. (1982). *Raising your hearing-impaired child: A guideline for parents.* Washington, DC: Alexander Graham Bell Association for the Deaf.

Madsen, C. K., & Madsen, C. H. (1972). *Parents/children/discipline: A positive approach.* Boston: Allyn & Bacon.

Meadow, K. P. (1968). Parental responses to the medical ambiguities of deafness. *Journal of Health and Social Behavior, 9,* 299–309.

Meadow, K. P. (1980). *Deafness and child development.* Berkeley, CA: University of California Press.

Mindel, E. D., & Vernon, M. (1987). *They grow in silence: Understanding deaf children and adults.* Boston: College Hill Press.

Mira, M. (1972). Behavior modification applied to training young deaf children. *Exceptional Children, 39*, 225–229.

Moses, K. L. (1985). Infant deafness and parental grief: Psychosocial early intervention. In F. Powell, T. Finitzo-Hieber, S. Friel-Patti, & D. Henderson (Eds.), *Educating the hearing-impaired child* (pp. 86–102). San Diego, CA: College Hill Press.

Naiman, D. W., & Schein, J. D. (1978). *For parents of deaf children.* Washington, DC: National Association of the Deaf.

Ogden, P. (1984). Parenting in the mainstream. *The Volta Review, 86*, 29–39.

Ogden, P., & Lipsett, S. (1982). *The silent garden.* New York: St. Martin's Press.

Paget, S. (1983). Long-term grieving in parents of hearing-impaired children: A synthesis of parental experience. *Journal of the British Association of the Teachers of the Deaf, 3*, 78–82.

Peterson, L. C. (1982). The child as a person. In *Parent education resource manual* (pp. 171–176). Washington, DC: Gallaudet University.

Proctor, A. (1983). Early home intervention for hearing-impaired infants and their parents. *Volta Review, 85*, 150–155.

Quigley, S. P., & Kretschmer, R. E. (1982). *The education of deaf children.* Austin, TX: PRO-ED.

Rodda, M., & Grove, C. (1987). *Language, cognition and deafness.* Hillsdale, NJ: Lawrence Erlbaum.

Rosen, R. (1986). Deafness: A social perspective. In D. M. Luterman (Ed.), *Deafness in perspective.* San Diego, CA: College Hill Press.

Schlesinger, H. S. (1985). Deafness, mental health, and language. In F. Powell, T. Finitzo-Hieber, S. Friel-Patti, and D. Henderson (Eds.), *Educating the hearing-impaired child* (pp. 103–113). San Diego, CA: College Hill Press.

Schlesinger, H.S. & Meadow, K.P. (1972). *Sound and sign: Childhood deafness and mental health.* Berkeley, CA: University of California Press.

Walters, R. P. (1982). Nonverbal communication in group counseling. In G. M. Gazda (Ed.), *Group counseling: A developmental approach* (3rd. ed., pp. 203–233). Boston: Allyn & Bacon.

Suggested Reading

Communication Choices

The American Annals of the Deaf. (Available from Gallaudet University, KDES, PAS 6, 800 Florida Avenue, NE, Washington, DC 20002)

Bornstein, H., Saulnier, K., & Hamilton, L. (1983) *The signed English dictionary*. Washington, DC: Gallaudet University Press.

Caccamise, F., & Drury, A. (1976). A review of current terminology in the education of the deaf. *The Deaf American, 29,* 7–10.

Carbin, C. F. (1976). A total communication approach: A new program for deaf infants and children and their families. *British Columbia Medical Journal, 18.*

Goldin-Meadow, S., & Feldman, H. (1975). The creation of a communication system: A study of deaf children of hearing parents. *Sign Language Studies, 8,* 221–236.

Henegar, M. E. (1971). *Cued speech handbook for parents*. Washington, DC: Gallaudet University.

Lawrence, E. D. (1979). *Sign language made simple*. Springfield, MO: Gospel House Press.

Ling, D. (1984). *Early intervention for hearing-impaired children: Oral options*. San Diego, CA: College Hill Press.

Ling, D. (1984). *Early intervention for hearing-impaired children: Total communication options*. San Diego, CA: College Hill Press.

Methods of communication currently used in the education of the deaf. (1976). London: Royal National Institute for the Deaf.

Pahz, J. A. (1978). *Total communication*. Springfield, IL: Charles C. Thomas.

Schwartz, S. (1987). *Choices in deafness: A parents' guide*. Kensington, MD: Woodbine House.

Spradley, T. S., & Spradley, J. P. (1985). *Deaf like me*. Washington, DC: Gallaudet University Press.

The Volta Review. (Available from the Alexander Graham Bell Association for the Deaf, 3417 Volta Place, NW, Washington, DC 20007)

Coping with Feelings

Bowe, F., & Sternberg, M. (1973). *I'm deaf too—Twelve deaf Americans.* Silver Spring, MD: National Association of the Deaf.

Featherstone, H. (1981). *A difference in the family: Living with a disabled child.* New York: Penguin Books.

Ferris, C. (1980). *A hug just isn't enough.* Washington, DC: Gallaudet University Press.

Fraser, G. R. (1976). *The causes of profound deafness in childhood.* Baltimore, MD: Johns Hopkins University Press.

Frederickson, J. (1985). *Life after deaf.* Silver Spring, MD: National Association of the Deaf.

Glick, F. P. (1982). *Breaking silence.* Scotsdale, PA: Herald Press.

Griffin, B. F. (1980). *Family to family.* Washington, DC: Alexander Graham Bell Association for the Deaf.

Harris, G. A. (1983). *Broken ears, wounded hearts.* Washington, DC: Gallaudet University Press.

Love, H. D. (1970). *Parental attitudes toward exceptional children.* Springfield, IL: Charles C. Thomas.

Luterman, D. (1987). *Deafness in the family.* Boston: Little, Brown.

Murphy, A. T. (1979). *The families of hearing-impaired children.* Washington, DC: Alexander Graham Bell Association for the Deaf (Special Issue of the *Volta Review*).

Naiman, D. W., & Schein, J. D. (1978). *For parents of deaf children.* Silver Spring, MD: National Association of the Deaf.

Schlesinger, H., & Meadow, K. P. (1976). Emotional support for parents. In D. L. Lillie, P. L. Trohanis, & K. W. Goin (Eds.), *Teaching parents to teach* (pp. 35–47). New York: Walker.

Culture

Batson, T. W., & Bergman, E. (Eds.). (1985). *Angels and outcasts: An anthology of deaf characters in literature.* Washington, DC: Gallaudet University Press.

Benderly, B. L. (1980). *Dancing without music: Deafness in America.* New York: Anchor Press/Doubleday.

The Deaf American. (Available from the National Association of the Deaf, 814 Thayer Avenue, Silver Spring, MD 20910)

Gannon, J. R. (1981). *Deaf heritage: A narrative history of deaf America.* Silver Spring, MD: National Association of the Deaf.

Higgins, P. (1980). *Outsiders in a hearing world.* New York: Sage Publications.

Holcomb, R. K. (1986). *Hazards of deafness.* Acton, CA: Joyce Media Publishing.

Jacobs, L. M. (1980). *A deaf adult speaks out* (rev. ed.). Washington, DC: Gallaudet University Press.

Lane, L. G., & Pittle, I. (Eds.). (1981). *A handful of stories*. Washington, DC: Gallaudet University Press.

Panara, R., & Panara, J. (1983). *Great deaf Americans*. Silver Spring, MD: T. J. Publishers.

Rosen, R. (1986). Deafness: A social perspective. In D. Luterman (Ed.), *Deafness in perspective* (pp. 241–261). San Diego, CA: College Hill Press.

Toole, D. K. (1981). *Courageous deaf Americans*. Beaverton, OR: Dormac.

Educational Placement

Brill, R. G. (1978). *Mainstreaming the prelingually deaf child*. Washington, DC: Gallaudet University Press.

The Broadcaster. (Available from the National Association of the Deaf, 814 Thayer Avenue, Silver Spring, MD 20910)

The Deaf American. (Available from the National Association of the Deaf, 814 Thayer Avenue, Silver Spring, MD 20910)

The Endeavor. (Available from the American Society of Deaf Children, 814 Thayer Avenue, Silver Spring, MD 20910)

Garretson, M. D. (1977). The residential school. *The Deaf American, 29*, 19–22.

Katz, L., Mathis, S., & Merrill, E. C. (1978). *The deaf child in the public schools: A handbook for parents*. Danville, IL: Interstate Printers and Publishers.

McAfee, J. K., & Vekgason, G. A. (1979). Parent involvement in the process of special education: Establishing a new partnership. *Focus on Exceptional Children, 2*, 1–13.

Nix, G. W. (1977). The rights of hearing-impaired children. *The Volta Review, 79* (Monograph).

A parents' guide to the IEP. (1978). Washington, DC: Gallaudet University.

Schimmel, D., & Fischer, L. (1987). *Parents, schools, and the law*. Columbia, MD: The National Committee for Citizens in Education.

Schwartz, S. (1987). *Choices in deafness: A parents' guide*. Kensington, MD: Woodbine House.

U.S. Office of Education. (1980). *Working with schools: A parents' handbook*. Government Printing Office No. 1980, 0-302-615. Washington, DC: Government Printing Office.

Hearing Aids

Blatchford, C. (1976). *Yes, I wear a hearing aid*. New York: Lexington School for the Deaf.

Cassie, D. (1976). *The auditory training book*. Danville, IL: Interstate Printers and Publishers.

Facts about hearing and hearing aids. (Available from the U.S. Food and Drug Administration, 8757 Georgia Avenue, Silver Spring, MD 20910)

The Hearing Journal. (Available from The Laux Company, Inc., West Bare Hill Road, PO Box L, Harvard, MA 01451; [617] 456-8000)

Jauger, J. S. *Orientation to hearing aids.* Washington, DC: Alexander Graham Bell Association for the Deaf.

Language Development

De Villiers, P., & de Villiers, J. (1979). *Early language.* Cambridge, MA: Harvard University Press.

Giddan, J., & Giddan, M. (1984). *Teaching language with pictures.* Palo Alto, CA: Consulting Psychologists Press.

Hillerich, R. L. (1986). *The American heritage picture dictionary (gr. K-1).* Boston: Houghton-Mifflin.

Larrick, N. (1982). *A parents' guide to children's reading.* Philadelphia: Westminster Press.

Ling, D., & Ling, A. (1977). *Basic vocabulary language thesauras for hearing-impaired children.* Washington, DC: Alexander Graham Bell Association for the Deaf.

Miller, A. (1974). *Your child's hearing and speech.* Springfield, IL: Charles C. Thomas.

Rudin, E., & Salomon, M. (1983). *My picture dictionary (gr. 1-3).* New York: Western.

Sheheen, D. (1984). *A child's picture English-Spanish dictionary (gr. K-6).* New York: Adama.

Whitehurst, M. W. (1971). *Teaching communication skills to the preschool hearing-impaired child.* Washington, DC: Alexander Graham Bell Association for the Deaf.

Miscellaneous Topics

Ambron, S. (1977). *Child development.* New York: Holt, Rinehart, & Winston.

Anastasiow, N. (1979). Current issues in child development. In A. Simmons-Martin & D. R. Calvert (Eds.), *Parent-infant intervention: Communication disorders* (pp. 3–12). New York: Grune & Stratton.

Baum, V. (1981). Counseling families of deaf children. *Journal of the Rehabilitation of the Deaf, 15,* 16–19.

Berrett, B., & Kelley, R. (1975). Discipline and the hearing-impaired child. *The Volta Review, 77,* 117–124.

Canter, L., & Canter, M. (1985). *Assertive discipline.* Santa Monica, CA: Canter.

Cohen, B. (1980). Emotionally disturbed hearing-impaired children: A review of the literature. *American Annals of the Deaf, 125,* 1040–1048.

Draper, M. W., & Draper, H. E. (1979). *Caring for children.* Peoria, IL: Charles A. Bennett.

Erikson, E. H. (1963). *Childhood and society*. New York: Norton.

Ferris, C. (1980). *A hug just isn't enough*. Washington, DC: Gallaudet University Press.

Forehand, R., Cheney, T., & Yoder, P. (1974). Parent behavior training: Effects on the non-compliance of a deaf child. *Journal of Behavior Therapy and Experimental Psychiatry, 5*, 281–283.

Freeman, R. D., Carbin, C. F., & Boese, R. J. (1981). *Can't your child hear?* Baltimore, MD: University Park Press.

Gelfand, D. M., & Hartmann, D. P. (1984). *Child behavior analysis and therapy* (2nd ed.). New York: Pergamon Press.

Gordon, I. J. (1979). Parents as teachers—What can they do? In A. Simmons-Martin & D. R. Calvert (Eds.), *Parent-infant interventions: Communication disorders* (pp. 13–30). New York: Grune & Stratton.

Gordon, T. (1976). *P.E.T. in action*. Ridgefield, CT: Wyden Books.

Graziano, A. M., & Mooney, K. C. (1984). *Children and behavior therapy*. New York: Aldine.

Griest, D. L., & Wells, K. C. (1983). Behavioral family therapy with conduct disorders in children. *Behavior Therapy, 14*, 37–53.

Harper, R., Wiens, A., & Matarazzo, J. (1978). *Nonverbal communication: The state of the art*. New York: Wiley.

Harrison, R. P. (1974). *Beyond words: An introduction to nonverbal communication*. Englewood Cliffs, NJ: Prentice-Hall.

Hasenstab, M. S., & Horner, J. S. (1982). *Comprehensive intervention with hearing-impaired infants and preschool children*. Rockville, MD: Aspen Systems.

Havighurst, R. J. (1972). *Human development and education*. New York: Longman.

Helleberg, M. M. (1981). Hearing impairment: A family crisis. *Social Work in Health Care, 5*, 33–40.

Kozoloff, M. A. (1979). *A program for families of children with learning and behavior problems*. New York: Wiley.

Krumboltz, J. D., & Thoresen, C. E. (1976). *Counseling methods*. New York: Holt, Rinehart, & Winston.

Kubler-Ross, E. (1969). *On death and dying*. New York: Macmillan.

Lillie, D., Trohanis, P. L., & Goin, K. W. (Eds.). (1976). *Teaching parents to teach!* New York: Walker.

Luterman, D. (1979). *Counseling parents of hearing-impaired children*. Boston: Little, Brown.

McCormick, B. (1975). Parent guidance: The needs of families and of the professional worker. *The Teacher of the Deaf, 73*, 315–330.

Morris, D., Collett, P., Marsh, P., & O'Shaughnessy, M. (1979). *Gestures*. New York: Stein & Day.

Murphy, A. T. (1979). The families of handicapped children: Context for disability. *The Volta Review, 5,* 265–278.

Neyhos, A. I., & Austin, G. E. (1978). *Deafness and adolescence.* Washington, DC: Alexander Graham Bell Association for the Deaf.

O'Dell, S. (1974). Training parents in behavior modification: A review. *Psychological Bulletin, 81,* 418–433.

Pahz, J., & Pahz, C. (1977). *Will love be enough? A deaf child in the family.* Silver Spring, MD: National Association of the Deaf.

Parent to parent resource catalog. (1984). (Available from House Ear Institute, 256 South Lake, Los Angeles, CA 90057)

Raffini, J. P. (1980). *Discipline.* Englewood Cliffs, NJ: Prentice-Hall.

Ross, A. O. (1981). *Child behavior therapy: Principles, procedures and empirical basis.* New York: Wiley.

Schmaman, F. D., & Straker, G. (1980). Counseling parents of the hearing-impaired child during the post-diagnostic period. *Language, Speech and Hearing Services in the Schools, 11,* 251–259.

Shontz, F. C. (1965). Reaction to crisis. *The Volta Review, 67,* 364–370.

Stein, L. K., Mindel, E. D., & Jabaley, T. (1981). *Deafness and mental health.* New York: Grune & Stratton.

Wadsworth, B. J. (1971). *Piaget's theory of cognitive development.* New York: David McKay.

Webster, L. M., & Green, W. B. (1973). Behavior modification in the deaf classroom: Current applications and suggested alternatives. *American Annals of the Deaf, 118,* 511–518.

List of Reinforcers

| *Circle the three items the child likes best of all.* |

1. Foods: _____

   _____

2. Drinks: _____

   Are there any foods or drinks child is allergic to? If so, please list:

   _____

3. Games or sports:

   _____ _____ _____

   _____ _____ _____

4. Toys:

   _____ _____ _____

   _____ _____ _____

5. Books (also, magazines, comic books, etc.):

   _____ _____ _____

   _____ _____ _____

6. Opportunities to be with others (e.g., parties, friends over, etc.):

   _____ _____ _____

   _____ _____ _____

7. Play with or care for animals:

   _____

8. Travel (parks, lakes, zoo, etc.):

   _____

9. Hobbies (collecting things, gardening, etc.):

   _____

10. Television (favorite programs):

    _____ _____ _____

    _____ _____ _____

11. Having a private room: Yes ☐   No ☐
12. Being left alone for a while: Yes ☐   No ☐
13. Helping around the house: Yes ☐   No ☐

(Adapted from Gelfand, D. M., & Hartman, D. P. (1984). *Child behavior analysis and therapy* (pp. 233–236). New York: Pergamon Press.

You and Your Hearing-Impaired Child

Behavior:			Period of Observation:	_____ Throughout Day _____ Part of Day From _____ to _____ (specify time)				
Sunday	Monday	Tuesday	Wednesday	Thursday	Friday	Saturday	Total	Dates

Behavior:			Period of Observation:	_____ Throughout Day _____ Part of Day From _____ to _____ (specify time)				
Sunday	Monday	Tuesday	Wednesday	Thursday	Friday	Saturday	Total	Dates

Behavior:			Period of Observation:	_____ Throughout Day _____ Part of Day From _____ to _____ (specify time)				
Sunday	Monday	Tuesday	Wednesday	Thursday	Friday	Saturday	Total	Dates

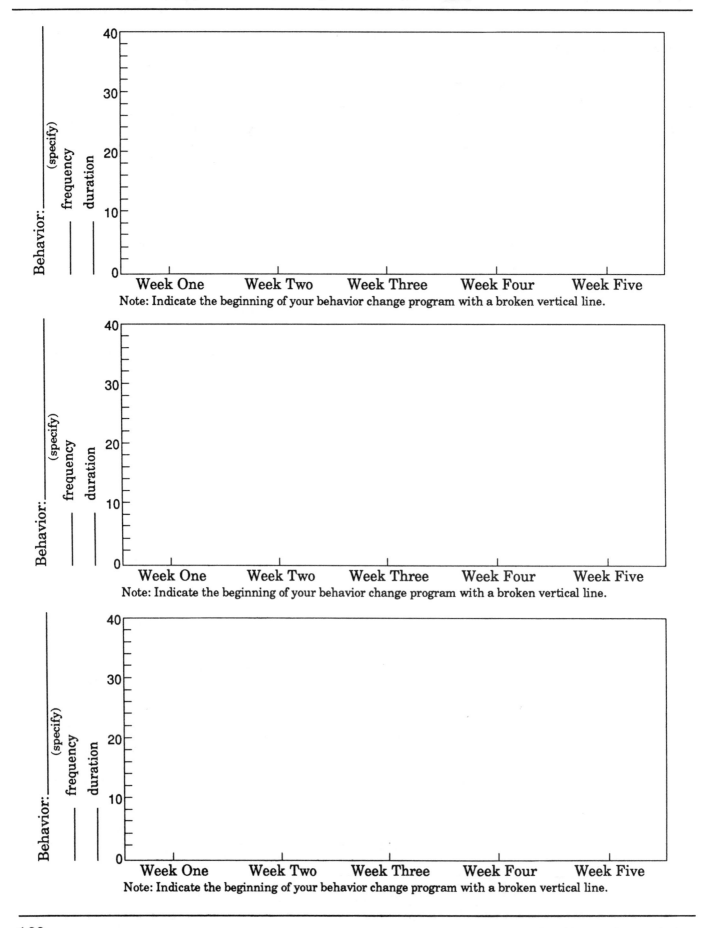

Behavior: _____ (specify)
_____ frequency
_____ duration

40
30
20
10
0
Week One   Week Two   Week Three   Week Four   Week Five
Note: Indicate the beginning of your behavior change program with a broken vertical line.

Behavior: _____ (specify)
_____ frequency
_____ duration

40
30
20
10
0
Week One   Week Two   Week Three   Week Four   Week Five
Note: Indicate the beginning of your behavior change program with a broken vertical line.

Behavior: _____ (specify)
_____ frequency
_____ duration

40
30
20
10
0
Week One   Week Two   Week Three   Week Four   Week Five
Note: Indicate the beginning of your behavior change program with a broken vertical line.

Comment Sheet

Please use back of page if necessary

Name: _____

Address: _____

_____

_____

☐ Parent   ☐ Professional _____
                                     (specify)

Are you using this book ☐ with professional supervision? ☐ without professional supervision?

☐ other _____
                                 (specify)

Comments: _____

_____

_____

_____

_____

_____

_____

_____

_____

_____

_____

_____

Return to: Dr. John W. Adams
                 Division of Behavioral Science
                 Rochester Institute of Technology
                 1 Lomb Memorial Drive
                 Rochester, NY 14623

Feedback and Answers

CHAPTER TWO
Activities for Practice

1. a. You may experience a variety of feelings while watching your child involved in certain activities throughout the day. For example, during playtime you may observe your child and experience a sense of peace and joy when seeing your child enjoy him/herself. However, at another time you may experience sadness. For instance, you may observe your child at resttime and begin to think about all the ways hearing impairment affects his or her life. Or, you may see your child with hearing children in the neighborhood and become angry about your child's hearing disability.

    b. Whatever the feelings you experience when observing your child, make note of them. This will help you in becoming more aware of the feelings you experience and the reasons for these feelings.

2. Parents express many different reactions to the discovery of the hearing-impaired condition in their child. Most parents share that this experience involves a great deal of adjustment and strength to cope with the changes in their lives. Most notable of the parents' descriptions of this period is the wide range of feelings that the diagnosis creates. Writing your personal thoughts about this part of your life can bring forth some of the same feelings that you experienced at the time your child's hearing loss was diagnosed. It is important to recognize that these feelings exist and that it is all right to experience them. Reviewing this aspect of your life can demonstrate to you the ways you have handled this difficult situation. Some parents say that they developed inner strength from this period in their lives.

    The diagnosis of hearing impairment in your child and the implications of hearing impairment on your child's life creates definite changes in your life and in your family. Writing this letter in this activity can give you the opportunity to reflect on how the hearing impairment has affected you. One parent shared this message in her letter: "We are finally growing stronger day by day. My husband and I are trying to be as supportive as possible to each other. We have our days, however. Sometimes I feel irritable and gloomy and my husband has to be the strong one. At other times, the situation is reversed. At any rate we are doing fine. We still have our moments, but what family doesn't?"

3. Individuals handle difficult situations in different ways. The way you handle an uncomfortable situation or difficult feelings is the way you cope. You may cope with the feeling of sadness or depression by sleeping. Or you may handle this type of feeling by making yourself busy with other activities to avoid focusing on the discomfort. You may use different ways to deal with each of the feelings listed in this activity.

Checking Your Progress

1. It is important not to ignore your child's comments and questions about hearing impairment. You can offer an explanation in language and terms the child understands. If no explanation exists, your child should be told and reminded how special, unique, and important he or she is.

2. a. True.

   b. False. The first stage of the grieving process, shock, involves feelings such as disbelief. Intense emotions such as anger, sadness, etc., are commonly experienced in the second stage, recognition.

   c. False. Feelings are neither good nor bad. They must be faced and dealt with according to your needs.

   d. True.

   e. False. Acceptance means you understand and accept the reality that your child is and always will be hearing-impaired. Acceptance is not happiness or contentment with the condition.

   f. True.

CHAPTER THREE
Activities for Practice

1. People cope with difficult feelings or situations in different ways. Reviewing the nine suggestions for coping with your feelings may give you ideas of different ways to deal with your particular circumstances. The final suggestion listed offers a few specific ways people use to cope. As you begin to think about ways to handle strong feelings, you may discover a new strategy for coping that can help you. Talking to others can help you to cope. Not only can speaking to someone about your feelings make you feel better, but you may discover additional ways of coping through another's suggestions.

2. Hearing impairment may affect you and your child's life in a variety of ways. For example, hearing impairment will affect how your child communicates with you. It may frustrate you when you cannot understand what your child wants or needs. A way to handle this feeling of frustration is to attempt to calm down before trying to communicate further. You might go into an area in the home free from distractions in order to focus primarily on the child

and his or her needs. Another way hearing impairment may affect you involves the limitations it places on your child. Even with a hearing aid, your child may hear some sounds and not others. When listening to music you may feel sad because you cannot share this experience with your child. You can cope with this situation by involving the child in experiences that both of you can share. Or, you may need to discuss these sad feelings with someone else.

3. Many parents have shared that the discovery of hearing impairment has a great impact on their lives. For example, during the diagnosis period, parents experience many different feelings such as sadness, anger, frustration, and confusion. In experiencing these feelings, parents discover different ways to cope that can be useful in the future. Some share that the handicapping condition has brought the family closer, enabling them to rely on one another's strengths. This experience also helps some develop a better understanding about the plight of those who belong to minority groups, including individuals with other types of disabilities, certain ethnic groups, etc.

4. If you do not know another parent with a hearing-impaired child you might need to contact your school district, a local audiology center, or other organizations to find out how to meet other parents of hearing-impaired children. Parent groups may meet at these locations and you may be able to contact other parents through support groups. Sources for parents are located in chapter eleven. Some of the organizations listed may provide you with information concerning how to meet parents of hearing-impaired children in your area.

Checking Your Progress

1. It is important to express how you feel about this situation. If feelings or emotions are strong, it would be wise to calm down before acting. One response may be to check your child's reaction to see if he or she can handle the situation on his or her own. It may be necessary to explain to your child that some people do not understand about being hearing-impaired, and they may act foolish because of their lack of understanding. If you are concerned about your child's reaction, you might distract your child from the situation by involving him or her in another activity.

2. a. False. Feelings can recur through your life and the life of your child. You will be reminded from time to time about the impact of hearing impairment.

   b. False. Feelings that are ignored could cause more difficult problems in the future.

   c. True.

   d. True.

   e. False. Parents can get in a habit of overprotecting their child, causing the child to develop an unrealistic view of the world.

f. True.

g. False. Feelings that are ignored can cause more difficult problems in the future.

h. True.

CHAPTER FOUR
Activities for Practice

1. a. Be very specific about the behaviors you observe; for example, Sam was very calm, he came home and wanted to rest in his room; Sue was extremely noisy, she threw and slammed her books on the table, slammed doors, yelled and screamed at her brothers and sisters, etc.; Charlie completed all of his homework, he was able to work for thirty minutes without a break.

   b. It is important for you to consider whether the behaviors in your child are age-appropriate or inappropriate. Use what you believe to be typical behavior at a particular age to judge if the behavior seen is appropriate.

      Examples: Three-year-old hearing-impaired child
         Behavior: Hitting others to get their attention
         (Age-appropriate, not unusual behavior for a child of this age)

      Ten-year-old hearing-impaired child
         Behavior: Hitting others to get their attention
         (Age-inappropriate, unusual behavior for a child of this age)

   c. As a parent of a hearing-impaired child, you must view your child's behavior in light of what is considered "normal" for all children. This will be helpful for several reasons. First, it can help you understand what is generally expected of a youngster your child's age. Second, you can compare the differences between what is expected and what behavior you observe. This can help you decide if the behavior is appropriate or inappropriate. Third, and most important, understanding what is expected gives you a starting point for determining what impact hearing loss has on your child. Even if you believe the behavior to be inappropriate, you may have a better understanding of why the behavior occurs. Developing an understanding can help you determine the best course of action to take.

2. When you are deciding on whether your child's behavior is age-appropriate or age-inappropriate, note whether the behavior is an ongoing pattern or if it has just recently developed. If the behavior has been occurring over a long period of time, it may be a habit or a part of your child's personality. If it is a new behavior, it could be a reaction to changes in your child's emotional, social, or physical growth. For example, a child reaching puberty may exhibit a variety of behaviors not seen before—irritability, mood swings,

acting-out behavior (e.g., fighting). A hearing-impaired child attending school for the first time may display behaviors such as crying or acting fearful or withdrawn.

New behaviors could indicate changes in your child's life. These changes may have helped cause the new behaviors seen. Being aware of how changes in growth can bring about changes in behavior can help you understand the behavior and perhaps aid you in deciding if it is appropriate or inappropriate.

Checking Your Progress

1. A tantrum is not age-appropriate for this child. This parent needs to set clear limits on the child's inappropriate behavior. However, this behavior may be related to problems in communication.

2. a. True.

   b. False. General patterns of behavior do exist, but should only be used as guidelines for our children's growth—not as a measure of whether specific behavior is normal.

   c. False. All children are unique individuals. Children may differ in their rates of development.

   d. True.

   e. False. Temper tantrums are quite typical for a two-year-old child.

   f. False. A ten-year-old is more relaxed and content than at previous age levels.

   g. True.

   h. True.

CHAPTER FIVE
Activities for Practice

1. See examples provided in the Activities for Practice section.

2. Parents of hearing-impaired children can use a variety of ways to convey limits to their children. It may be helpful to show or demonstrate the limit to your child. For example, while your child is sitting at the dinner table, you can show him or her appropriate behavior. You can also demonstrate unacceptable behaviors, following this with another demonstration of what is expected. Some parents find it helpful to devise a picture book to illustrate the limits (e.g. a toy box drawn with toys scattered on the floor around it, arrows drawn from the toys pointing toward the toy box). The pictures contained in the picture book serve as visual reminders of rules and limits.

3. You need to follow through on rules and limits consistently. If you are not consistent in giving the consequences you have decided upon, your child can become confused and believe the limits are

not important. All children will occasionally test limits. You must place consequences on your child's behavior when the limit is followed (reward or reinforcement) and when it is not followed (punishment, ignoring, etc.).

Checking Your Progress

1. You need to set limits on your child's behavior. For example, you may decide that the chores must be done before your child can receive some reward. Your limits should be stated in positive, clear terms and followed up on consistently.

   Example of limit: All chores must be completed before leaving the house.

2. a. True.

   b. False. All children need to know limits of their behavior. These limits help them make sense of their world.

   c. True.

   d. False. Limits need to be specific to behavior in order to let the child know what to expect.

   e. True.

   f. True.

   g. False. The hearing-impaired condition has definite impact for setting limits on behavior. Limits must be explained clearly and explicitly.

   h. True.

CHAPTER SIX
Activities for Practice

1. Parents differ in what they believe to be misbehavior in children. One parent may perceive his or her child making loud noises as misbehavior, and another may not find this behavior troublesome. On the other hand, many parents may consider refusal to do what a child is told to be defiant and inappropriate behavior. Only you can define what you believe to be misbehavior in your child. You must also examine the response you give your child when he or she misbehaves. Your response will generally determine whether your child's behavior will continue. For example, if your child consistently does not do the chores you request around the home, your response is critical to the child's future behavior. You can ignore the child's behavior or act on it by acknowledging the misbehavior and providing an appropriate consequence (such as taking away certain privileges, or rewarding the child when chores are done correctly).

   Although there is no one right way to respond to your child's misbehavior, you can determine if your response was effective by examining your child's future behavior.

2. This activity helps parents to look more closely at their interactions with their children. It is helpful to recall as much of the interaction involving the misbehavior as possible. It may be worthwhile to do several A-B-C patterns involving situations where the behavior occurs only occasionally. You may then see the types of responses or consequences that encourage the child to continue the behavior. For example, if a child seems to fight with other children or argue with adolescent peers, you might apply the A-B-C pattern on several occasions when this behavior occurs. You may discover some similarities in each of the situations that is encouraging your child's behavior to occur. In completing the A-B-C pattern over time, you may see that your youngster has trouble interacting with others when involved in games or structured activities. This type of situation requires the child to follow rules. Perhaps the antecedent event is that the child does not know the rules or how to follow the rules consistently, and this has led to the child's difficulty in interacting with his or her peers. Or, perhaps the child is getting attention due to his problematic behavior during these activities.

3.

A Antecedent	B Behavior	C Consequences
Sam's demanding occurs in and out of the house; more intense in public. Demanding seldom occurs with father. Demanding occurs when mother doesn't respond to his requests.	Sam demands that his mother give or buy him things. When mother does not respond, Sam gets angry, and shouts and screams.	Mother interacts with Sam a lot when the demanding occurs. She pleads and begs Sam to stop. Sometimes she gets tired and gives in.

Checking Your Progress

1.

A Antecedent	B Behavior	C Consequences
Johnny doesn't like homework. Teacher has not received homework. Television in room. Papers torn-up.	Watching TV. Not doing homework.	Watching TV is fun. Getting out of homework.

Recognizing this pattern is helpful in understanding what encourages the child's behavior. Antecedents and consequences contribute to misbehaviors. For example, having a television in the room where the child is supposed to be doing homework (antecedent) entices the child. The child receives pleasurable outcomes (consequences—enjoying TV, relaxing without doing homework) for the behavior.

2. a. True.

   b. True.

   c. False. These words are too vague and do not indicate specific behaviors. They may hold various meanings for different people.

   d. True.

   e. True.

   f. False. Using the A-B-C pattern has been proven to be effective with hearing-impaired children. This pattern does not rely on language to be successful.

   g. True.

   h. True.

CHAPTER SEVEN
Activities for Practice

1. Listed below are examples of child behaviors seen by parents and how they might decide to measure them.

Behavior	Frequency (How often?)	Duration (How long?)
a. Use of polite behavior	√	
b. Fighting behavior	√	
c. Amount of time it takes to do chores		√

2. This is an example of a measurement of a child's behavior to examine how often or how long it occurs. This parent also made a graph of the time it took her child to get ready for school during a two-week period.

Behavior: *getting ready for school*   Period of Observation: ____ Throughout Day   √ Part of Day
From 7:00 A.M. to 8:00 A.M. (specify time)

Sunday	Monday	Tuesday	Wednesday	Thursday	Friday	Saturday	Total	Dates
	44 min.	35 min.	32 min.	38 min.	40 min.			5/8-5/12
	50 min.	42 min.	40 min.	35 min.	38 min.			5/15-5/19

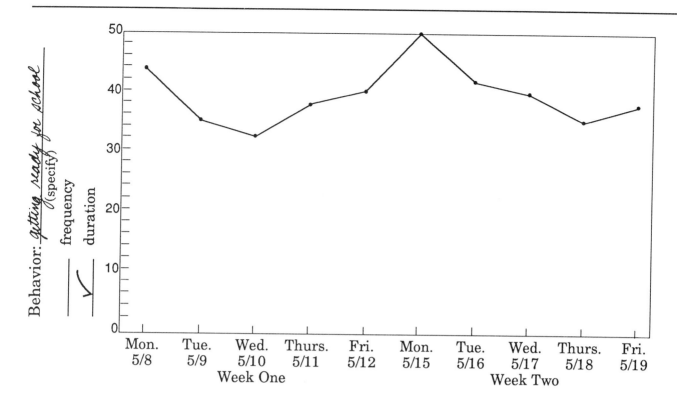

Behavior: *getting ready for school* (specify)
✓ frequency
___ duration

3. Measuring your child's behavior at the beginning is only a first step in your plan to change behavior. You must then decide on which antecedents and consequences are needed to change your child's behavior. You should continue to measure the behavior in the weeks to come to see if the new antecedents and consequences helped change your child's behavior.

For example, you would like to change your child's talking-back behavior. You measure the frequency (how often) of the behavior as it occurs during two weeks. These are your results:

Behavior: *talking back*				Period of Observation:	___ Throughout Day			
					✓ Part of Day: After School			
					From 3:00 P.M. to 5:00 P.M. (specify time)			
Sunday	Monday	Tuesday	Wednesday	Thursday	Friday	Saturday	Total	Dates
///// //	/////	///// ///	///// /	///// ///	///// /	///// /////	50	Week 1

After measuring the talking-back behavior for a week, you decide on the antecedents and/or consequences you would like to change.

For example, when your daughter talks back you will ignore her comments and take away one privilege she was given for that week (going to friend's house, watching television, etc.). Also, you will reward her good response and communication behavior by letting her choose a fun activity following several good responses.

After placing these consequences on her actions consistently, you should continue measuring the talking-back behavior. You may see these results:

Behavior: *talking back*	Period of Observation:		Throughout Day						

Behavior: *talking back* **Period of Observation:** ___ Throughout Day √ Part of Day: After School From 3:00 P.M. to 5:00 P.M. (specify time)

Sunday	Monday	Tuesday	Wednesday	Thursday	Friday	Saturday	Total	Dates
///// //	/////	///// ///	///// /	///// ///	///// /	///// /////	50	Week 1
///	//	//	/////	///	/	/////	21	Week 2
/		//	//	/		/	7	Week 3

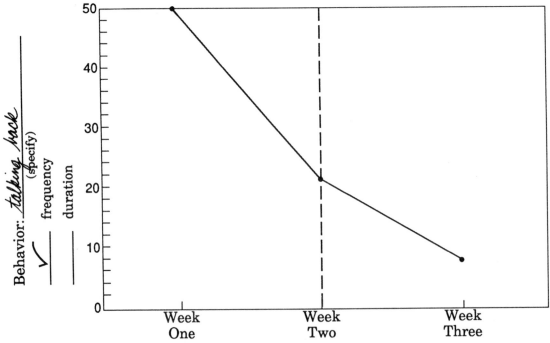

Behavior: *talking back* (specify) √ frequency ___ duration

Note: The broken vertical line indicates the beginning of the behavior change program.

It is obvious that your plan is working because your child's talking-back behavior is decreasing.

Continue to measure your child's progress until you are confident that the behavior has changed.

Checking Your Progress

1. a. Specify behavior: David teases his sister; calls her names;
        threatens her with hitting behavior.

    b. How will you measure the behavior?

        __X__ Frequency   _____ Duration
              (How many)   (How long)

    c. When will you observe the behavior?

        _____ Throughout day   __X__ Part of day
              (happens infrequently)   (happens frequently)

        __3:30 P.M.__   to   __4:00 P.M.__   after school
                           (Specify time of day)

    d. Possible response: I will observe David playing with his sister
        at playtime. I will record how many times David teases his
        sister throughout this half-hour.

2. a. False. The first step in changing behavior is to observe
        the behavior.

    b. True.

    c. True.

    d. False. Using time out is removing the child from a situation
        that is reinforcing.

    e. True.

    f. True.

    g. False. It is very important to help a child learn appropriate
        behaviors to replace inappropriate behaviors. A child should
        be rewarded for appropriate behavior so it continues.

    h. True.

CHAPTER EIGHT
Activities for Practice

1. Nonverbal behaviors add meaning to the verbal message. It is
    difficult to imagine our communications with others without the
    use of facial expressions, eye contact, and body language.

2. Individuals use various nonverbal behaviors to convey their
    messages. Just as different people use different nonverbal
    behaviors to convey messages, different people may read different
    nonverbal communications differently. You can try this exercise
    to illustrate this point. Try to demonstrate these feelings to
    another person using only facial expressions: hostility, concern,
    and boredom. Check to see if the other person can select which
    feeling you are attempting to convey. This activity, similar to
    that of Activity 2, will help demonstrate the power of nonverbal
    behaviors in conveying messages. Also, behaviors may be read
    differently by different people. Being aware of nonverbal behaviors

will help you recognize the importance of these messages to your child. Being aware of nonverbal behaviors and their impact on communication will also help you read your hearing-impaired child's nonverbal cues.

3. This activity helps you be more aware of the use and the importance of nonverbal language in our communication system. You can discover a great deal of information about others through their use of nonverbal behaviors. Picking up on nonverbal behaviors, however, is not easy. We are used to communicating verbally. We are not as practiced in using our vision to determine a message. We need to develop the skills of interpreting and using nonverbal behavior like any other skills. Practice is important. Practice exercises will help you become more aware of nonverbal communication and its use.

4. Your child will rely on nonverbal communication much more than his or her hearing peers. It is therefore important to actively practice techniques to enhance your skills in nonverbal communication. For example, getting down to your child's eye level to communicate will help him or her see your facial expressions and eyes, which provide vital information concerning your messages. When using the techniques suggested in chapter eight, observe if your child responds better during your interactions. Continue to use these techniques and practice these methods consistently when you interact with your child.

Checking Your Progress

1. Mary's father's nonverbal behavior is inconsistent with the message he wants to communicate. Also, the father's business associates are reinforcing Mary's behavior by saying "Isn't she sweet!" Finally, attention is reinforcing Mary's behavior.

2. a. True.

   b. True.

   c. True.

   d. False. Nonverbal cues supplement and enhance verbal communication. These cues can clarify the spoken word.

   e. True.

   f. False. Nonverbal communication is effective with verbal language.

   g. True.

   h. True.